UNDER
THE
BANYAN TREE

The Forgotten Story of Barrackpore Park

Monabi Mitra
Soumen Mitra

AAKAR

UNDER THE BANYAN TREE
The Forgotten Story of Barrackpore Park

Monabi Mitra & Soumen Mitra

First published in 2019
by
AAKAR BOOKS
28E, Pocket IV, Mayur Vihar,
Phase - I Delhi 110091
INDIA
www.aakarbooks.com

ISBN 978-93-5002-621-2

Disclaimer :

The findings / views / opinions expressed in this book are solely those of the authors and do not necessarily reflect the views of the publisher.

Cover illustration : Edward Lear
Cover design : Ranajit Basu

Printed by : Capital Infoart Private Limited, INDIA
www.capitalinfoart.com

FSC

This book has been crafted using FSC certified paper

For
Ranita Gupta & Sushen Mitra
Keepers of tradition past and future

Barrackpore, January 1874
Edward Lear landscape drawings, MS Typ 55.11, MS Typ 55.26
© Houghton Library, Harvard College Library

CONTENTS

ACKNOWLEDGEMENT

Our special thanks are due to Professor Nandini Gooptu, Professor Swati Chattopadhay and Anabel Loyd for invaluable help in accessing archival collections; to Timothy Melgund, 7th Earl of Minto for permission to publish family photographs; to Lord Lansdowne and The Trustees of the Bowood Collection; to Micah Hoggatt of the Houghton Library, Harvard Unversity, Malini Roy of the British Library, London and to Jennie Rayner of the Sydney Living Museums for their help in licensing material we needed; to Satish Chandra Tewari, IAS, Secretary to the Governor of West Bengal for his support in using the archives of Raj Bhawan, Calcutta; to Dr. Jayanta Sengupta, Secretary and Curator of Victoria Memorial Hall, Calcutta, for retrieving material from the rich holdings of the Victoria Memorial Hall and its archives; to G. M. Kapur of INTACH, always an invaluable optimist to anyone who is aware of the compelling need to restore and conserve old buildings; to Nikhil Kapur, who generously lent a hand in photographing the gardens and buildings of Barrackpore Park; to Manish Chakraborty, architect and consultant of the West Bengal Heritage Commission for the restoration project at Barrackpore; to the many representatives of Harewood House, England, the National Library, Calcutta, Metropolitan Museum, New York and the Asiatic Society, Calcutta who corresponded with us and aided our acquisition of supplementary data; and finally to Ranajit Basu, Nila Paul and the late Sanjib Chakraborty of Capital Infoart for preparing the manuscript.

Countless other persons worked tirelessly to restore the built heritage of Government House, Barrackpore from 2017. This book is a tribute to them and to all the unknown people who toiled and built the Government House and its adjoining parkland in the past.

FOREWORD

The first Lord Minto, Governor General of India 1807-1813 wrote: 'Barrackpore is delicious and takes the sting out of India'. When I first visited Government House, Barrackpore, more than ten years ago, I was editing the Indian Journal of his great granddaughter-in-law, Mary Minto, Vicereine of India from 1905-1910. Like many of her predecessors, in particular Harriot Dufferin and Ava who also wrote of her Indian life, Lord Curzon who wrote about everything, and Charlotte Canning, the first Vicereine, who recorded her years in India in letters, journals and most notably in her accomplished watercolours, Mary loved the weekends and Christmases at Barrackpore that gave her and her family a literal breath of fresh air after the weekly round of official life in Calcutta. The huge, high-ceilinged rooms of the house hardly fit the average weekend cottage mould for most people but for her and its earlier chatelaines, sitting in the glorious tropical exuberance of its surroundings, breakfast promised under the great banyan tree and a sense of holiday informality in the air, Barrackpore brought echoes of country life at home, of revival, relaxation with friends, and most of all, a garden to which each occupant in turn might add her own inspiration.

By the time I saw the house and the garden, the long unpainted Lady Hardinge Bridge over the weedy Moti Jheel leading to broken gates and into the landscape of melancholy decay described by Mark Bence-Jones as long ago as 1967, nature's exuberance untended had long since tangled and overwhelmed visions of past pleasure. It seemed inevitable the 'crumbling ruin' of the house too would soon succumb entirely to encroaching nature or to the wreckers' ball, to ugly new buildings and the wiping clean of another unwanted historical slate. How astonishing then the different and progressive vision embodied today in the ongoing restoration work at Government House and throughout the Barrackpore estate implemented by Soumen and Monabi Mitra.

Cavernous rooms are filled with noise as teams of workmen rebuild, repoint, plaster and paint and there is that familiar sense, conjured in the passages and pavilions of former palaces and stately homes around the world, of the people who once lived there. They have just stepped outside, gone on holiday, are temporarily elsewhere while the builders make and mend. They are documented down the generations by the Mitras in 'Under the Banyan Tree', their detailed history of Barrackpore and its occupants, so we may look forward with them towards the revival of the Park, Government House and the various bungalows and cottages still in existence as a resource for the present and to its continuing and evolving value for generations to come.

The ghosts lately raised in Government House; the sweeper on that old spiral staircase behind the bathrooms; Lord X frozen at his desk; Lady Y at her easel or her ease under a shady tree; they are from that foreign country, the past. We are all part of our own and the global historical narrative; the determined or determinedly neglectful destruction of bricks and mortar has rarely buried the ills of history or successfully forced its better fit with a different time and view, and neither should it. The best we can do is to use and exploit the memories and relics of our complicated shared heritage to inform, educate and enrich the present in the always hopeful anticipation of lessons learned and improved futures. That is the task Soumen and Monabi Mitra have taken on.

As they write in the penultimate chapter of this book, Barrackpore was always synonymous with 'the fragility of Indo-British relations', the revolts of both 1824 and 1857 broke out in this quasi anglicised environment. The re-placing of the memorial to Mangal Pandey in its proper place near the gatehome at Barrackpore as opposed to incorrectly inside the former Viceregal garden is a highly important part of the restoration work in hand. All those statues of British rulers standing silent among the bright dahlias at Flagstaff House, the classical cenotaph built there in the garden by the first Lord Minto, they are also part of the long long history of India that has encompassed and absorbed invaders from the Persians to Alexander the Great and the Mughals to the British.

'Under the Banyan Tree' gives a picture of a part of the lives of the most privileged among the 'colonial masters'. Their days may be recent enough for livid scars to remain but the concrete residue of their existence can do no harm. Instead, the best purpose for the restitution of their one-time exclusive pleasure grounds and houses is to become the remarkable repository of history and nature and the recreational resource for all its visitors that is envisaged by the Mitras and illustrated by this book.

If Barrackpore lost its first importance as a weekend retreat when the Government of India began to spend the hot months in Simla, it was increasingly forgotten once that unwieldy machine moved to Delhi long before the final days of the Raj. Its neglect thereafter due to lack of money or interest of successive governments and for all the resultant losses to its built estate, may have added considerably to the value of its natural heritage. For new generations aware of climate change, loss of habitat, the resulting depletion of flora and fauna and living inside the massive metropolitan area of Greater Kolkata it can become once again an extraordinary oasis.

Happily, the Barrackpore menagerie described with its sad captives in 'Under the Banyan Tree' is long gone and the days of such animal collections may truly be consigned to the past. On the other hand, while Emily Eden's Chinese pheasants no longer strut in the aviary, indigenous birds and insects depicted by the painter Sita Ram two hundred years ago and by Dr Francis Buchanan, surgeon-naturalist to the East India Company, still fly overhead, perch in the trees, wade in the shallows of the Hooghly and creep through the hidden parts of untouched jungly garden. Their ubiquitous kin, the hawks that once amused visitors by swooping down for pieces of meat during lunches in the garden, are still there with screaming flocks of parakeets. The nimble descendants of jackals, used in different times to attempt dognapping of small foreign pampered pets, still watch and wait in the undergrowth to see what will happen next.

Anabel Loyd

PROLOGUE

The night was dark and we were tired. Our road ran on past crowded byways and clamorous streets till it turned left and passed in through a gatehouse into softer, greener land. We wound through the grounds of the State Police Academy, passing whitewashed buildings and broken balustrades. A waning moon shone dimly upon us; crickets buzzed in the trees and bats flitted here and there.

And then, suddenly through the bleakness we saw the sharp edges of a rectangular building looming up ahead. Someone lit a flashlight and we ascended a broken flight of stairs. Inside was a cavernous room, and then another and still another. Here and there, through the beams of the tungsten light that criss-crossed the dusty floors, we could discern vague shapes: tin trunks, hospital beds and a mound of rotting rags.

Past these lay a darkness which an imaginative mind could easily fill with sombre gowns and cheerful bonnets, breeches, caps, gleaming uniforms and turbaned figures of dark tan.

❦

This is the story of Government House, Barrackpore: once the Governor General's weekend retreat, later the Viceroy's quick getaway and then a Police Hospital after Independence, languishing in disrepair and slowly passing out of public memory.

The life of this magnificent building is inextricably entwined with the lives of those it housed. While the Viceroys laboured away at the gruelling task of running a government on what was essentially foreign soil, from cities like Calcutta, Madras and Bombay, Barrackpore served as a respite from the tumult of daily life. It is not surprising, therefore, that this building exists not so much in official records as in personal letters and diaries, many of which we will use for reference.

Ours is not the first chronicle, nor, it is hoped, the last. Partly a tribute, partly a restoration project, partly a hearkening to a time when laughter echoed through these corridors and music drifted out of these walls, the following pages show how connections can be made across different worlds and over long centuries.

Barrackpore, December 1873
Edward Lear landscape drawings, MS Typ 55.11, MS Typ 55.26
© Houghton Library, Harvard College Library

INTRODUCTION

"

"Today Barrackpore has lost much of its original character.
The house is used as a police hospital.
The great drawing room is a typhoid ward. . . ."

Splendours of the Raj
British Architecture in India, 1660 – 1947
Philip Davies

"

The Hoogley - from the Course - Calcutta [1857-1858]
Dominick Sarsfield Greene
© Caroline Simpson Library and Research Collection, Sidney Living Museums

Government House, Barrackpore
© European Architecture in India 1750–1850
Sten Nilsson

The British empire in India fulfilled itself in many ways. Forged by a trading company, fattened on the native economy, fortified by an army, strengthened by its civilians and bureaucracy, it was sustained by an elaborate ceremonial culture of display and magnificence. The buildings of Empire served the needs of circumstance as well as of pomp and show. Seventy-two years since independence and the crumbling of Empire, we can still see its footprints in an assortment of Company and Raj era constructions that remain scattered throughout the country. Hospitals, court houses, cantonment houses, bungalows, schools and colleges, government offices and quarters, hotels, railway stations, churches, cemeteries, bridges and clubs, the list is endless.

This book charts the story of one such building, the Government House at Barrackpore, which began as a twin of its counterpart in Calcutta before quite inexplicably passing out of public memory. Beginning as a weekend retreat for the Governor General in 1801, the fortunes of the Barrackpore Government House rose and fell till 1947 when it was handed over by a newly independent government to the West Bengal Police. In time it was forgotten.

In the new millennium there was even talk of demolishing this odd decaying mansion which had vague heritage value but not much else. Its park was overgrown and scrawny, newly constructed houses had come up in a slap-dash manner on its grounds and historical inaccuracies had muddled its past. The banyan tree in the south garden which had served as a centre of recreation for the Viceroys and their families was confused with a similar tree in the Cantonment where Mangal Pandey, sepoy of the 5th Company of the 34th Regiment Native Infantry had been hanged. He had brandished a sword and loaded musket, calling out to all the other sepoys to assemble against the new greased cartridges which would make them lose religion, thereby triggering a round of mutinous disorder that rippled through large portions of British territory and was known as the Revolt of 1857.

Around that time Barrackpore cantonment became synonymous with a new mood in Indian politics. It began to symbolise a location of opposition and dissent for the Indians while the British viewed it as an epicentre of violence and inglorious mutiny. In the meanwhile Simla had been discovered and built upon. The British withdrew to Simla for a large part of the year, while Barrackpore Park remained the weekend country house, a quick journey from Calcutta and suitable for a day or two.

Once the capital was shifted from Calcutta to Delhi there was a decline in fortune. After India's independence in 1947, Government House was converted into a police hospital with a few pieces of rudimentary medical equipment. Interest in the house shrank further after the introduction of private medical facilities in the service whereby hospitals outside the campus became the regular choice. At the time this book began to be written, the house clung to its hospital nomenclature in a roundabout way and functioned as a barrack for police personnel on sick leave who were unable to go home.

East India House, London
Thomas Malton the Younger
© Metropolitan Museum, New York

It is therefore somewhat startling to realize that the mansion that once sheltered giants and was used as the second home of redoubtable figures like the Lords Moira, Amherst, Dalhousie, Auckland, Canning, Dufferin and Curzon to name a few, is now a lonely crumbling ruin of peeling walls and sorry neglect. Meanwhile the residence of the Private Secretary to the Governor General, also known as the Flagstaff House, is the official country retreat of the West Bengal Governor today. Its lawns are strewn with statues of British administrators, removed from Calcutta for being disturbing reminders of a colonial past. This adds to the puzzle; many believe that Flagstaff House was the original Viceregal house. Furthermore, New India, for whom the colonial experience is a remote historical fact rather than a lived reality, cares little for Government Houses, real or pretended. To them Eden Gardens is a cricket stadium rather than a garden built by Lord Auckland and Wildflower Hall near Simla is a swish hotel rather than the site of Lord Kitchener of Khartoum's summer palace!

For lovers of history the East India Company's expansion in India is a fascinating story. Beginning as a mercantile power it suddenly found it had the running of a large tract of the world in its hands. In its early years, between 1757–1820 the Company was engaged in frequent wars for establishing English rule on a sure footing in India. The emphasis was on revenue collection. Hence military campaigns and territorial accession were undertaken for the privilege of trade as well as the safeguarding of these privileges.

Yet, though the English East India Company had paramount power over many Indian states in the 18th century, this power was exercised by keeping up the charade of Mughal sovereignty and paying lip service to the Mughal Emperor living as a pensioner in Delhi. In time rampant corruption amongst the Company's servants made the British Parliament bring Company rule increasingly under the control of the Government through an organization known as the Board of Control. By 1833 the Charter Act took away the Company's monopoly over Indian trade and enjoined a more responsible kind of governance. As time went on the British became all-powerful through a spate of wars and collisions with regional forces. In the treaties which the defeated Indian powers were made to sign, the British established themselves as supreme. As they triumphed, they pushed in a little further with their cultural and architectural practices. The process of creating urban centres as in Calcutta, Bombay and Madras was thus part of the British impulse of creating a recognizable 'colonial' space, a kind of mini-Europe that put a familiar stamp on an otherwise unfamiliar landscape.

View of Government House, Calcutta, 1794
William Baillie
© Caroline Simpson Library and Research Collections,
Sydney Living Museums

When the English East India Company set up their factory in Calcutta the administrators had to make do with huts made according to local building techniques. These were usually mud huts with thatched tops, preferred by the earliest agents as cheap to build. These mud-built thatched houses were the nucleus of the city of Calcutta in the 17th century.

Gradually a self-contained English factory was built. In time a Fort was added to provide security for the factory though this fort was also built in the indigenous way, what Captain Hamilton in 1727 describes as 'brick and mortar called puckah, which is a composition of brick-dust, lime, molasses, and cut hemp, and when it comes to be dry, is as hard and tougher than firm stone or brick.'[1]

After the Mughal emperor Farrukh Siyar in 1717 granted permission to the East India Company to purchase the zamindari rights of twenty four villages besides the three of Sutanuty, Gobindapur and Kalikata, which they already held, rights had been legally established and the merchants felt secure enough to begin construction of brick-built terraced houses, surrounded by gardens. The three villages themselves grew into a thriving town. This new town was a cosmopolitan dream, with a diverse population of Europeans and Indians. Everyone had begun to flow to Calcutta, including the British, Portuguese, French, Armenians, Jews and Chinese. A church called St. Anne, dedicated to the reigning queen had been built on the site of the western end of the future Writers' Buildings while a hospital functioned in what was later Garstin Place, close to where the buildings of the High Court stand today. The Europeans preferred to function from the Fort and except for the Church and this hospital, all other buildings including barracks, factors'

houses, warehouses, workshops and the Governor's house stood densely packed together within the Fort.

The Governor also enjoyed the luxury of a private dwelling outside the walls, with a wider garden and a more salubrious air near where we have today's Bankshall Court. A raised road running from the Fort marked the outer margin of the settlement. This cut through the marshy waste of Bow Bazar Street to the creeks and salt lakes of the East where boats filled with produce from the jungles unloaded their wares for the burgeoning population of the new town.

The siege of Calcutta by Nawab Siraj-ud-daullah and the sack of the city, followed by Clive's victory against the Nawab's army in March 1757 and the subsequent recovery of the city by the British, is a tale that belongs to another telling. The Governor's residences, both within and outside the Fort were in ruins after the siege. It is possible that the original Governor's House was burnt down by the Nawab, which is why, of all the three Presidencies, Government House, Calcutta is the newest. Subsequent dwellings are obscure and difficult to pinpoint. In 1774 the Governor General Warren Hastings lived in an official house that was modest in comparison to his stature. So too did his successors.

The early buildings of the East India Company were built for military defense, trade, religious practices and the most rudimentary requirements of domestic living. Focussing on an expansion of territories with a view to dominate trade, this was clearly not a time of extravagant show. Ostentation and pomp were condemned. Ironically, though, the man sent out to increase the fortunes of the

Company, Lord Wellesley, was also the one who began the architectural job of Empire.

Just as Wellesley peremptorily annexed vast swathes of Indian territories and brought them under Company rule, he also attempted to increase British stature and establish its superiority by creating a grand architectural heritage. By building a palatial residence for the Governor General in Calcutta and beginning another one at Barrackpore, Wellesley's motives were the exact opposite of Company policy. The Company was a money making mercantile organization, but Wellesley had an imperial vision and it was necessary for him to duplicate territorial expansion with gigantic effect. In order to achieve ruling status by transforming, reordering and creating a new space, Wellesley sought to create visual markers that would reflect a superior ethos.

Before Wellesley's new house, references to a Government House speak of a plain building. The French traveller M. Grandpré in 1789 describes a large house on the Esplanade as belonging to the Governor, which was 'by no means equal to what it ought to be for a personage of so much importance;'[2] this house, as shown in a painting by Baillie in 1794, shows a humble house of two storeys, with a closed verandah on the upper floor, a balustrade terrace and a single room on the roof with a sloping top. There was also a courtyard flanked by two square pillared gateways opening on to the Esplanade. Too small to be used for official entertainments, contemporary accounts state how the Governor used the Court House, the social hub of Calcutta society for such purposes.

Meanwhile a New Fort was nearing completion south of the Old Fort which by then was deemed as unsuitable, both for being too shallow from attack as well as too uncomfortable a reminder of the Black Hole tragedy. Grandpré describes both in his account. The site of the Black Hole was marked by a pyramidal monument standing upon a square pedestal, with sculpted designs on each side and inscriptions in 'the English and Moorish languages, describing the occasion on which it was erected. The Old Fort is an indifferent square, with extremely small bastions, that can mount at most but one gun, though the sides are pierced for two.'[3]

The need for re-making Calcutta was realized by all, and the Court of Directors in their Proceedings of 1764 agreed 'to build a new Council Room at a convenient distance from the offices'[4] and selected a site open to the breezes of the river and near the New Fort. This was to be the official residence of the Governor. Once the house was made, it was clubbed together with another house bought by the Company from the estate of a deceased gentleman named Richard Court. These two houses were used for the official residence of the Governor till 1799.[5]

In 18th century India, the British architects who created early public buildings were not trained in their craft as a cadre of professional architects but were usually civil or military engineers, used to constructing barracks, rest houses, courts, hospitals and post offices rather than lofty designing. In Calcutta, famous civil engineers included John Garstin (1756 - 1820) and the chief civil architect Edward Tiretta (1726 - 1806) followed by Richard Blechynden (1759 - 1822). All these men took the lead in designing public buildings. But Wellesley chose to ignore them and appointed military engineers to present designs for Government House, Calcutta as well as the one in Barrackpore possibly

Grand Entrance to the Government House Calcutta, 1850
Captain R. B. Hill
© Gilman Collection, Metropolitan Museum Purchase, 2005

because military engineers were keen to take on additional commissions to supplement their pay and took care to keep civil engineers out of the way. A stream of Chief Engineers who served the army planned major buildings of the British settlements including Captain John Brohier, who re-designed Fort William on French models and Charles Wyatt who belonged to a prestigious family of eminent architects. Wyatt used Kedleston Hall, Derbyshire as a model for his own design of Government House, Calcutta because his uncle Samuel Wyatt had worked on the house in England. This was in keeping with the mood of these early engineers who used European models for their architectural blueprint and built many Indian buildings along British models.

With its round central dome, lofty gates and colonnaded frontage Wellesley's Government House made an excellent centerpiece in early Calcutta. A contemporary writer wryly described it as 'that noble edifice, the seat of Government and Wellesley's pride.'[6]

To the north of Government House was the 'respondentia' or what the area between Chand Paul Ghat and Government House was known as, possibly because this was the place where shipping insurance was secured. Between the 'respondentia' and Fort William, Chowringhee on the east and the river on the west, construction was forbidden and the space was kept open to allow the Hooghly breezes to cool the city and add a pleasant effect.

As Calcutta developed so did the cantonment at Barrackpore. Indeed Barrackpore cantonment has the distinction of being the oldest such in the country. By the time Clive had destroyed Siraj-ud-daulah's army at Plassey he had shifted his attention from Madras to Fort William in Calcutta, realizing perhaps the importance of curbing the powers of the other European factories in Bengal. The Danes had grouped at Frederiknagar, later known as Serampore, the Dutch at Chinsurah, the French at Chandernagore and the Portuguese at Hooghly.

Plan of the Park at Barrackpore as reconstructed by the authors

N

The
Barrackpore
Cantonment

RIVER HOO

Legend

1. Government House
2. Lady Canning's Terrace / Lotus Fountain
3. Lady Ripon's Bamboo Tunnel
4. Middle Landing Ghat
5. Semaphore Tower
6. Flagstaff House
7. Flagstaff
8. Cenotaph
9. Band Master's Bungalow
10. Cook's Room
11. West Gate
12. Moti Jheel
13. Lady Hardinge Bridge
14. Bungalow no. 1
15. Staff Quarters
16. Bungalow no. 2
17. Honeymoon Lodge
18. Guard Room
19. Cook Room
20. Meat Room
21. Kitchen
22. Banyan Tree
23. Tennis Court
24. Lady Lytton Borders
25. Myall King's Grave
26. Lady Jackson Rose Garden
27. Aviary Tank / Lily Tank
28. Old Aviary / Fern House
29. Seed House
30. Curzon Minto Rose & Vegetable garden
31. Serpentine Lake
32. Lady Canning's Tomb
33. Site of Wellesley's Government House
34. Band Stand
35. South Gate
36. Eden School
37. Deer Park
38. East Gate
39. Coachman's Bungalow
40. Menagerie
41. Mali's House
42. Golf Links
43. Park keeper's House
44. Dairy
45. Minto Fountain
46. North Gate
47. Lord Ellenborough Avenue
48. Lord Elgin's Bamboo Tunnel
49. Horse Shoe Lake
50. Minto Garden
51. Bamboo Gate
52. Lower Landing Ghat
53. Upper Landing Ghat
54. Church
55. Flower Garden
56. Elephant Stall
57. Governor General's Stables
58. Green House
59. Mahogany Avenue

Barrackpore Trunk Road

To Calcutta

G H L Y

Clive built cantonments all along the Ganges and the Hooghly, at strategic positions, in Danapur, Berhampore, Dum Dum and Barrackpore. There was the need to keep an eye on the Nawab at Murshidabad because the sack of Calcutta had come as a huge shock to the Company, which had been unprepared for such a situation.

Barrackpore cantonment had come up on the old Indian village of Achanok. It was near Chandernagore and thus convenient for keeping an eye on the French from across the river. Ordnance factories had come up on adjacent sites at Cossipore and Icchapore. Once the cantonment was set up around 1775, directions from Fort William decreed that the military headquarters of the Presidency Division be set up at Barrackpore under a Commander-in-Chief. Accommodation for the Commander-in-Chief was duly approved and a house purchased for his use. This was the estate that Wellesley appropriated in 1801 for building a weekend retreat. Once built, the delight of the house was its garden and the surrounding park. Lord Wellesley had cleared swamp and jungle to free up almost 350 acres of land. This was landscaped into low hillocks and mounds giving it the appearance of rolling parkland. Other lords and lady sahibs brought in their own inspirations. Lady Canning made an Italian garden surrounded by a balustrade with brilliant poinsettia arching over. The First Earl of Lytton built a stone staircase in the south verandah. Lady Ripon planted a bamboo tunnel on the walk and brought in a rose garden, as also erecting a porch in front of the house. The second Lord Elgin had installed a sundial at the southern entrance. Lady Minto inaugurated a fountain amidst a private garden in the south in the early 20th century.

As a country retreat the house was lavished care and loved by most of the Governors General. Though there was no permanent domestic staff, bands of servants were sent on ahead to make the house ready when a family visit was planned. One could travel to it by carriage on the straight road cutting across the flat Calcutta hinterland from Calcutta to Barrackpore, as built by Lord Wellesley himself, or one could take the romantic route along the river, in the luxurious state yacht known as the *Soonamookie*, a wonderful houseboat accompanied by a flotilla of barges carrying four hundred or so servants for the Lordship's needs. In the 20th century the Viceroy could also motor from Calcutta, though this became increasingly dangerous in the ignited atmosphere of the Freedom Movement.

With the buildings of the two Government Houses, at Calcutta and Barrackpore, the British sought to create an architectural precedent. While Government House, Calcutta was the lofty seat of Empire, Barrackpore was the private realm - a cozy enclave where the rulers could withdraw from the ruled and decide policy matters as well as enjoy privacy. Its rolling gardens and spacious landscaped settings were a deliberate contrast to the crowded chaotic native parts as well as British Calcutta, overrun by private mansions and administrative buildings.

The geometrical layout at Barrackpore, of the house and the park, was an expression of British superiority: its ordered landscape an externalization of Western rationalism and a conscious departure from the native. It was also what has been described as a deliberate implanting of the grandeur of an imperial order upon the mundane operations of mere trade, especially the indigo and muslin trade which were extremely oppressive and the only mode of sustenance for the Empire.

Above all it was a hybrid space, a point where home and the foreign met. The river that flowed by was tropical, broad and meandering and dotted with barges and boats plying busy trade. In the evening the sun set upon a sultry land which was beautiful in spite of the heat, one in which the parakeets screeched, clouds of fireflies hung about the shrubs and jackals howled angrily in the park. But the House was stately classical, its inhabitants were primed by the imperial task in hand and for a while at least there was an assurance that the British had supreme mastery over this great and exciting land. All the wonders of this tropical luxuriance lay at their command. As Emily Eden, never one for empty sentimentalizing put it, 'but there was a lovely moon, and the Hoogly is a handsome bit of river, and we floated about for an hour, and then went to bed.'[7]

Government House, Barrackpore has been the subject of travellers' tales from the 19th century, has figured in chapters on books tracing the architectural heritage of the British in India and has been fondly remembered in memoirs and letters of British rulers and their wives. But time is ruthless and memory is short. The 19th and 20th centuries are over and today, touching the second decade of the 21st century, there are palpable signs that the House has passed into an Ozymandias - like situation. Though still too early to say 'nothing beside remains'[8], there is a need to hearken back to the past and give the house a new lease of life.

This book hopes to bring together available material on the origin, building and history of Government House, Barrackpore as a tribute to a two-hundred-year old legacy. By doing this it is hoped that seventy-two years after British rule the ghosts of the imperial past are laid to rest. British rule has become part of the shared history of India and its architecture endures as a palimpsest of Bengal's history.

❧

NOTES ————————————————————————

1. Blechynden, Kathleen. 1905. Calcutta Past and Present. Thacker, Spink & Co.
2. Grandepré, L. 1803. A Voyage in the Indian Ocean and to Bengal Undertaken in the Years 1789 and 1790. Vol II. G and J. Robinson. London.
3. Ibid.
4. Losty, J.P. 1990. Calcutta City of Palaces: A Survey of the City in the Days of the East India Company 1690 - 1858. The British Library.
5. Ibid.
6. D'Oyly, Charles. 1828. Tom Raw, The Griffin: A Burlesque Poem, In Twelve Cantos: Illustrated By Twenty-Five Engravings, Descriptive Of The Adventures Of A Cadet In The East India Company's Service, From The Period Of His Quitting England To His Obtaining A Staff Situation In India. R. Ackermann.
7. Eden, Emily. 1919. 'Letter to Mr C. Greville, Barrackpore, April 17th, 1837.' Miss Eden's Letters. Macmillan and Co. Edited by Violet Dickinson.
8. Shelley Percy Bysshe, Ozymandias.

CHAPTER ONE

THE BEGINNING

"

"The regal palace, on fair Hooghly's stream,
Slumb'ring he passes, the green shelving shore
Dotted with trees, that in the sunshine gleam,
With varied hues of blossoms studded o'er"

Tom Raw, The Griffin: A Burlesque Poem, in Twelve Cantos
Charles D'Oyly

"

View of the Governor's House Barrackpore, 1800
© RIBA Collections

Wellesley's constructions at Government House, Calcutta and the garden house at Barrackpore show the same forceful determination, shrewdness and disregard for established norms that helped him enlarge British territories in India. His political policy, the Subsidiary Alliance, was a devious artifice by which Indian rulers were made to bind themselves to unnecessary military alliances while ceding their sovereignty. In architecture as well, he cunningly outsmarted the Directors of the East India Company in London and proceeded to build two palaces that endure till today.

Mystery reigns over Barrackpore's Government House from the start: over its construction, site, legality and expenses incurred. Wellesley began the train of events by enshrouding its existence in a fog of muddle in an attempt to prevent the masters of the Company from interfering in his building plans, possible in those days due to ill-developed communication. What is certain from the earliest written records of the house is that it was connected to the cantonment.

The cantonment at Barrackpore had come up on the old settlement of Achanok, a prosperous village dating back to the 15th century. When the cantonment sprang up at Barrackpore around the middle of the 18th century, bungalows built by Englishmen began to proliferate. Some of the first buildings to be built in the new cantonment area of Barrackpore were two thatched bungalows for Captain John Macintyre. Macintyre sold his property in 1785 to Sir John Macpherson, acting Governor General, for a sum of about 3000 pounds.[1]

This property, which measured almost seventy acres, was acquired for becoming the garden house of the Commander-in-Chief. The succeeding Governor

Barrackpore Park
© The British Library Board

General, also Commander-in-Chief, was Lord Cornwallis who however, did not appear to have used the property at all. John Shore, Governor General from 1793-98 was not the Commander-in-Chief and thus could not use it. In 1798 Richard Wellesley was appointed Governor General and he brought about a sharp change in the fortunes of the house.

Much of what Wellesley did was different from things done before. When he arrived in Calcutta with a sumptuous array of stores, baggage and

Barrackpore Park, Barrackpore Menagerie
© The British Library Board

Barrackpore. The Seat of the Governor General 16 miles from Calcutta
Charles Ramus Forrest, 1807
© British Library Board

carriages valued at 2000 pounds, he created quite a sensation. In the words of the irrepressible William Hickey whose *Memoirs* are full of delectable tidbits of contemporary Calcutta life, 'Lord Mornington arrived there in the Virginie frigate, at once bursting forth like a constellation in all his pomp and splendour amongst us.'[2]

In 1800, the new Governor General decided to take over the house of the Commander-in-Chief for a garden house that would belong solely to the Governor General. He used elaborate arguments to prove that the house 'has accidentally passed into the hands of the Commander-in-Chief, and that it is resumable at the pleasure of the Governor General in Council.'[3] Eager to move in before the upcoming hot season, Wellesley was also keen to gain control of the house and its precincts forever. Fortuitously, the then commander, Sir Alured Clarke, was due to return to England and Wellesley in 1801 officially transferred the rights of usage of the bungalow from the military administration to the Governor General-in-Council. In a letter to a friend in June 1801, Wellesley describes more candidly how he has been 'residing almost entirely at Barrackpore, a charming spot, which, in my usual spirit of tyranny, I have plucked from the Commander-in-Chief.'[4]

View of Calcutta, 1794
William Baillie
© Caroline Simpson Library & Research Collection, Sydney Living Museums

William Hickey in his memoirs describes how this happened: 'Not content with having works of such magnitude and unbounded expense on foot, he at the same time commenced a second palace at Barrackpore almost rivaling in magnificence the Calcutta one, which he intended as a country residence for future Governor Generals as he could not expect it would be completed within his own reign.'[5] Alured Clark's house was in poor shape and could hardly satisfy Wellesley's ambitious plan. Captain Charles Wyatt was appointed to repair it. As the palace was getting on, a new temporary bungalow was erected. This is the building that was enthusiastically described by Lord Valentia, who embarked on an ambitious tour of the East including India, accompanied by his secretary Henry Salt. It was described as 'a light-coloured villa with an Ionic portico, around which several smaller buildings are arranged.'[6]

Valentia adds that the waters were clearer than in Calcutta. The river was filled with the state barge and cutters of the Governor General, painted green and gold and presenting a scene of immense splendour. The house appears in its first look in a black and white sketch by Henry Salt, showing the thatched bungalows and the classical pillars.

Wellesley ordered the house to be surrounded by a rolling park for which he made significant alterations to the ground, digging up the earth, creating ponds, making an undulating landscape and planting a variety of trees for the new garden. To add to the homely English effect the Baptist Church of St. Olaf at Serampore, on the opposite bank, was inducted into the picture with the addition of a steeple, towards which Wellesley contributed 10000 rupees.

In spite of the repairs to the Commander's building Wellesley was dissatisfied. Something grander, more luxurious had to be done in keeping with the majesty of the Government House, Calcutta which was completed in 1803 at a cost of 63,291 pounds. Thomas Anbury, who had succeeded Wyatt as superintendent of public works was enlisted for the

Vignette: The Governor General's Seat at Barrackpore 1803
Henry Salt
© Voyages and Travels to India, Ceylon and the Red Sea
Lord Valentia, 1809

On The Terrace at Barrackpore, 1828
© British Library Board

task. The old bungalow was pulled down and plans made for a new one. A sum of four lakh rupees was sanctioned to construct the new Government House. Construction began shortly and a plinth was made. A temporary residence was built further up the river to act as an interim one. A balustrade bridge was made over the Moti Jheel, one of the water bodies in the Park which stands till today.

By an order of August 1801, Wellesley also acquired land for building a straight road linking Shyambazar Bridge in North Calcutta to Barrackpore. The new road was named the Barrackpore Trunk Road. Trees were planted on either side to provide shade and carts were forbidden to ply on the sides of the road lest the newly planted trees were destroyed. Wellesley had decided that once the house was complete all public offices would be shifted from Calcutta to Barrackpore for the duration of the Governor General's residence.

A series of semaphore towers were built along this road to serve as watchtowers. In times of danger, coloured lights could be used as signals to convey messages, necessary in those times when telegraph was yet to be installed. Three such towers were built along the road from Calcutta to Barrackpore and the one in the Park stands tall till this day.

Beyond his duties of governance and expansion, Lord Wellesley had an interest in scientific research. This drew him close to Dr. Francis Buchanan, a surgeon-cum-naturalist of the East India Company who was commissioned to undertake surveys of Nepal, Mysore and Bengal. Buchanan used the opportunities of travel and information collection that a survey entailed to collect plant specimens, drawings and create a valuable database of flora and fauna in the Company's lands. Wellesley had found a kindred spirit in Buchanan and made him his personal physician as well as the Director of the Natural History Project of India which he set up in Barrackpore. The aviary and the menagerie of Barrackpore park were made part of this project. The birds and beasts housed there had been procured for the proposed Department of Natural History at Fort William College. The department never saw the light of day and the samples were transferred to Barrackpore. Lord Wellesley and Dr. Buchanan came together in Barrackpore to pursue a rhinoceros and rare birds. No doubt Wellesley had hoped to add to his specimens. In 1813, almost eight years after he left, an English traveller named Maria Graham who visited Barrackpore mentions seeing pelicans, storks, flamingoes, ostriches, two tigers and two bears in the menagerie.

In 1805, Lord Wellesley was abruptly recalled to England. In spite of his victories in Mysore and his territorial advances, there was a general feeling that he had overstepped himself. The Court of Directors were tired of his extravagant motives and wished no further expense. 'We learn', they said, 'notwithstanding the heavy expense incurred on account of the Government House at Calcutta, that a building of considerable extent has been commenced at Barrackpore for the residence of the Governor General; this too at a time when our finances are in a state of the utmost embarrassment...'[7]

His successor, Lord Cornwallis (re-appointed Governor General in 1805) died soon after arrival but had been briefed to be prudent with the Company's purse. Sir George Barlow who was acting as Governor General from 1805 to 1807 had also been ordered not to proceed with such ambitious and expensive schemes. Yet Barlow managed to bring in some measure of closure by enlarging the temporary house and converting each corner of the verandahs into rooms.

This makeshift house would become the Government House, long after Wellesley's original plan was done away with. A water colour by Edward Hawke Locker in 1808 shows the Governor General's villa at Barrackpore with its familiar parkland, the small canal called the Moti Jheel with a bridge over it and the broad reach of the river in

Richard Wellesley

their shared love of scientific methodology. Buchanan had long hoped to be chosen as a successor to William Roxburgh in the very coveted post of Director of the Botanic Garden in Calcutta where one could pursue botanical research in a relatively free atmosphere. The Barrackpore post, he thought, would perhaps be an important step in that direction.

The menagerie was hoped to begin a systematic study of zoology by identifying, classifying and observing birds and quadrupeds of South Asia. The animals were housed in cages, of Gothic and Classical styles. A variety of animals was displayed including tigers, leopards, monkeys, bears, a giraffe,

The Governor General's House at Barrackpore, 1808
Edward Hawke Locker
© The British Library Board

the distance. Beyond this Barlow could do nothing for fear of angering the Directors.

The general tenor of the East India Company, from first to last, had been cruelly unsentimental and commercial. Aesthetics, amusements and architectural aggrandisement were all frowned upon. Later in the 1840s, Emily Eden in her letters plaintively recounts how countless presents made to the Governor General had to be auctioned off and converted into money for Company coffers. The East India Company had no illusions about the raison-d'etre of its existence. It

was there for successful trade and had no grand delusions of according to itself a sense of imperial destiny. After Wellesley's departure, all work stopped. The materials for the aborted building were taken to Calcutta, where all the beams, doors and windows were auctioned by the first Lord Minto. A large quantity stored in a depot in Calcutta was destroyed in a fire. The project seemed to have come to naught.

So stood the unfinished mansion in Barrackpore, ruinous and abandoned, when Maria Graham, on a visit to Barrackpore describes how the moonlight

A View of Serampore from the Park at Barrackpore 1826
© Trustees of the Victoria Memorial Hall, Calcutta

over the heaps of stones gave a romantic air: 'We landed at the palace begun by the Marquess Wellesley, but discontinued by the frugality of the Indian Company; its unfinished arches shewed by the moon-light like an ancient ruin, and completed the beauty of the scenery.'[8] It was only during the time of the Marquess of Hastings who would be Governor General from 1814–1823 that the unfinished work would be resumed and the temporary house would be completed as the weekend retreat.

Wellesley's attitude to architecture had been very different from that of his predecessors. Whilst the latter had looked upon their tenures in India as brief and reckless sojourns to swell coffers and return to England, Wellesley was touched with the architect's vision of leaving signs of permanence in an otherwise transient world. In Calcutta he undertook town planning by creating new road alignments and in 1803 an Improvement Committee was set up whose duties were to ensure that streets and lanes should be constructed in a systematic and orderly manner. This would later merge with the Lottery Committee of 1817 in which funds for expanding Calcutta were raised through lotteries. The Government Houses at Calcutta and Barrackpore were part of this systematic reordering and modernization of Calcutta from a city huddled anyhow around a fort to a sophisticated metropolis.

WIlliam Munnew or Munnoo and William Hickey, 1819
William Thomas
© National Portrait Gallery, London

Wellesley also set the tone for an important aspect of British governance. This was the creation of visual panoply as reminders of imperialism and to serve as metaphors for British superiority. Certainly, from an administrative standpoint he had worked hard at it—taking on the mighty Marathas and the hitherto invincible rulers of Mysore. Hyder Ali and his son Tipoo Sultan were defeated and subjugated while the Marathas were reduced in might. It was the Marquess of Hastings who finally took their capital Poona over into British territory.

Wellesley's plan for creating imposing structures as official residences had symbolic impact, an assertion of British might and the creation of a distinctive colonial culture. Thus it was that the classical lines of Government House, Calcutta were sought to be duplicated in the weekend retreat of Barrackpore. In both sites the construction was predominantly of Greco-Roman forms, with their elegance, symmetry and order a reminder of cultured Europe and in stark contrast to the crowded, riotous and profuse Indian styles.

Government House, Calcutta was built in imitation of Kedleston Hall in Derbyshire, the seat of the Curzon family and built in 1759. The house in Barrackpore was also built along the lines of the English manor house and incorporated elements from a typically English garden. With its green lawn, parkland, streams, menagerie, and bungalows scattered around the Park it had the effect of a peer's private house. The house was created to be a place for recreation and private social life away from the formalities of Calcutta. Privacy, indeed, was a constant focus of British architecture in the colonies. While the latticed verandahs, slatted windows, rattan screens, high walls of a compound, enormous gardens and long gravel walks that typified

Marquess Wellesley at the Nabob of Oudh's Breakfast
Sir Charles D'Oyly
© Heritage Image Partnership/Alamy Stock Photo

a British bungalow commanded the sense of an unapproachable entity, their public buildings conveyed arrogance and a sense of assurance. The new house at Barrackpore as Wellesley envisaged it was to be a lordly affair, a fitting reminder of England's supreme force as well as being a retreat from the cares of Calcutta society and politics.

Jan Morris has described in her impressive account of the architecture of the Raj, how the buildings expressed the will of the British rulers, not simply to evangelize, rule or exploit another, but also to adapt itself to utterly alien circumstances. In climates

Barrackpore Park
Sir Charles D'Oyly
© Trustees of the Victoria Memorial Hall, Calcutta

unfamiliar and demanding the buildings were attempts to survive as well as create an imperial effect.[9] And so, as their military successes increased, up came all over India a host of chapels, bungalows, grand houses for the Residents, palaces for the Governors and Governor General, barracks, forts, cantonments, clubs and colleges, in styles as diverse as Palladian, Georgian, Gothic, and the hybrid Indo-Saracenic of the 20th century.

The Barrackpore house was built in fits and starts from 1800 onwards but once it had assumed its final shape it was looked upon with affection by its inhabitants. All loved it as a counterpart of the English country house, situated as it was on the banks of a broad river, surrounded by a shady park, with the reassuring visual of a church steeple on the opposite bank. But Company rule had its contradictions. Although it vastly increased in territorial might after easily subjugating native rulers as well as other European powers like the Danes, the French, the Portuguese and the Dutch, its essence was that of a mercantile organization. Lavishness was discredited, economizing encouraged. Hickey summarized the situation admirably as he dryly describes the very different modes of conveyance that the out-going and incoming Governor General enjoyed. 'Lord Wellesley in a coach and six, preceded and followed by a party of Dragoons and out-riders while ten minutes afterwards I likewise met our new Governor General, Marquess Cornwallis driving himself in phaeton with a pair of steady old jog-trot horses.'[10]

Between pomp and parsimony, the Company clearly favoured the latter. Lord Wellesley was caught in a bind between his vision of what imperial India ought to have and the Company's very practical idea of what a profitable trading body ought to be. A century later Lord Curzon would face the same problem.

NOTES

1. Curzon, George Nathaniel (The Marquis Curzon of Kedleston, KG) 1925. British Government in India - The Story of the Viceroys and Government Houses, Volume Two, Cassell and Company
2. Hickey, William. 1925. Memoirs of William Hickey Vol. 4. Hurst & Blackett Ltd. Edited by Alfred Spencer.
3. Choudhry, Shantonu. 1995. 'Letter from Lord Wellesley to the Commander-in-Chief dated 1800." History of Barrackpore Cantonment: The Oldest in India. Station Headquarters, Barrackpore.
4. Ibid.
5. Hickey, William.
6. Valentia, George - Viscount. 1809. Voyages and Travels to India, Ceylon, the Red Sea, Abyssinia and Egypt in the Years 1802, 1803, 1804, 1805 and 1806. Miller London.
7. Choudhry, Shantonu.
8. Graham, Maria. 1813. Journal of a Residence in India. George Ramsay and Company.
9. Morris, Jan. 1983. Stones of Empire: The Buildings of the Raj. Oxford University Press.
10. Hickey, William.

CHAPTER TWO

ARCADIA

"

*"On Monday evening I go to Barrackpore, and remain there till
Friday morning, when I return at five o'clock a.m. by water to
Calcutta, and am there soon after seven. This division of the
week, besides making half of it delicious, is of real advantage to
business. At Barrackpore I can read, and really do so the livelong
day."*

Lord Minto in India: Life and Letters of Gilbert Elliot, first Earl
of Minto from 1807 to 1814
Edited by the Countess of Minto

"

On September the 15th, 1807, Lord Minto, or Gilbert Elliot, First Earl of Minto to give him his full title, had arrived in India after a four-month voyage on the *Modeste*, manned by his elder son Gilbert Elliot. He was to take up the post of Governor General from Sir George Barlow, the acting Governor General. Minto had landed at Madras, been met by his close friend Lord William Bentinck as well as his third son John Elliot, a writer promoted to be the Private Secretary of his father. Ten days before a brief uprising of sepoys at Vellore had been quelled and peace reigned once again.

Lord Mino had come to India after a round of rapid change. Lord Wellesley had been replaced by an aged Cornwallis for a second tenure, but Cornwallis had died within months of arriving in India and was buried at Ghazipur, overlooking the River Ganges. There was now a need for some one reliable to rule over the Company's fortunes. Minto, friend of Edmund Burke and one of the managers in the trial of Warren Hastings had been chosen over Barlow to govern India.

From the start official work bored Lord Minto. He had left his wife behind in Scotland and so the lack

George Barlow
Unknown Artist
© National Portrait Gallery, London

Lord Cornwallis
Thomas Gainsborough
© National Portrait Gallery, London

of family made him lonely. While Wellesley, during his stay in India was preoccupied with plans of expansion and acquisition, Minto was conservative and maintained a policy of consolidation. Wellesley's family life was erratic and though he corresponded regularly with his long-time mistress-turned-wife Hyacinth Gabrielle, whom he had left behind in London, they were separated upon his return to England.

Lord Minto was more of a family man and clearly pined for his wife throughout his stay. He was also a quiet man of simple tastes, very different from the flamboyant Lord Wellesley, with his unconventional ways and unorthodox style of governance. Minto's secretaries with their mountains of notes, their bundles of correspondence and dispatches wearied him and the need to meticulously go through it all, give orders and take decisions on the spot was tiresome. It was a strain to hear the droning voice, the *punkah* swinging heavily over the hot, clammy room and he writes of heroic efforts made to keep his attention from wandering. It is no small wonder then that the wide park and fresh river breeze of Barrackpore invigorated him and induced real pleasure. In Calcutta the Government House was cavernous and imposing, but ceremoniously so with elaborate rituals established by his predecessor. The customary morning and evening drive, though extravagantly

Gilbert Elliot, 1st Earl of Minto
© National Portrait Gallery, London

muslin gowns crowded into his dressing room, not the comely maidens he had hoped for but turbans and burly black beards. Doors were kept open, the partitions were transparent and all could hear and see one another. More beards and turbans slept in the passages, sepoys guarded all the doors and staircases, *salaaming* and giving him quite a turn when he stirred out of his room. 'I have gradually got rid of all this troublesome nonsense, but enough remains and must remain to tease me and turn comfort out of the doors,'[2] concludes Lord Minto, though despairing of his son John who *is* 'Orientalized already and is mighty content to have five fellows attend his toilet.'[3]

The fact was that Minto's experiences clashed heavily with European notions of privacy. The classic home in Britain had evolved from the 18th century to small, self-sufficient rooms, a profusion of corridors and separate entrances and exits for servants. The taste was for withdrawal and solitude where books could be read, conversations made, letters could be written and minds enlightened. The British manor house, from which the Mintos came, was architecturally built around segregation with curtained beds, bell-pulls for domestics, arbours in the gardens and recesses everywhere. The elite of Britain treasured and honoured privacy. Coming from such a culture it must have been a shock to conform to the Lord Sahib's milieu built around the openness of the Orient where private and public spaces were effaced.

Unlike in the Calcutta house, in Barrackpore Lord Minto found privacy, as did many of his successors. Though forced by the Company to put off further construction, he was admiring of the place nevertheless. In his words 'The present house is what is called a bungalow or cottage, and was intended

done, was a nerve-wracking affair, almost a pageant with an officer and six troops as bodyguards, four syces with horse flappers running alongside the horses, Europeans saluting, natives swarming up and touching the ground with their heads. It was no better in a palanquin ride where he had to be heralded by servants carrying gold and silver maces, halberds, embroidered fans, some proclaiming his title as they ran along 'which, as the proclamation is rather long, I imagine must be Hindostanee for Gilbert Elliot, Murray of Melgund, and Kynyumound of that ilk.'[1]

At night the fanfare increased and at bedtime there were further domestic excitements. On his first night in Calcutta fourteen persons with white

A llama and a pair of monkeys at Barrackpore Park
© British Library Board

only as a makeshift while the great house was erecting. It is a cottage, indeed, but a very considerable building compared with the European scale. The bungalow was originally composed of three large rooms, which opened into a verandah surrounding the whole. Sir George Barlow, by converting each corner of the verandah into a small room, has greatly improved the comfort of the house. The verandah next to the room is a charming apartment. It affords a long, shaded, airy walk with a most beautiful prospect, and we find it an excellent eating-room. It is within forty or fifty paces of the water's edge.'[4]

Wellesley's temporary bungalow was gradually morphing into the originally conceived palace, or at least an approximation of it. Though Minto applauds the architecture of the bungalow, this was a paradox because the bungalow was one of the most troubling aspects of European architecture Indianised. With an open-plan structure, privacy was again difficult to obtain as rooms opened onto rooms, the verandah was a public space and the high ceilings were a contrast to the cozy British middle-class home.

Yet perhaps the First Earl of Minto warmed to Barrackpore because it gave him an illusion of being back in England. Exiled from Britain in the job of creating Empire this was also to be a recurring motif for all succeeding residents. After describing the

Fighting at Java
Unknown Artist
© British Library Board

'neat Swiss cottages scattered about the lawn'[5] for housing aide-de-camps and guests, he wonders momentarily whether Wellesley's projected palace should have been completed. 'It would have been magnificent.'[6]

But then again it would spoil the real intent of Barrackpore if it was to have the same servants and socializing. 'It would have been to come from Calcutta to Calcutta again.'[7] The modest house, spacious but not palatial was desirable. In 1807, Minto describes how the grounds were a mixture of parkland and pleasure-ground with varieties of trees and shrubs 'whose rich verdure covered the tops with the river flowing busily past.'[8]

In 1811 Lord Minto headed a ten thousand strong expedition to Java to preempt the expansionist plans of Emperor Napoleon who had instituted a Franco-Dutch government in Java. After the victorious British had slaughtered half the Dutch army, Stamford Raffles was appointed Governor of Java for five years. Both Minto and Raffles worked hard for humanitarian reforms including the abolition of slavery. In August 1812 Raffles, also a great naturalist and biologist, reciprocated their

Sir Thomas Stamford Raffles
George Francis Joseph
© National Portrait Gallery, London

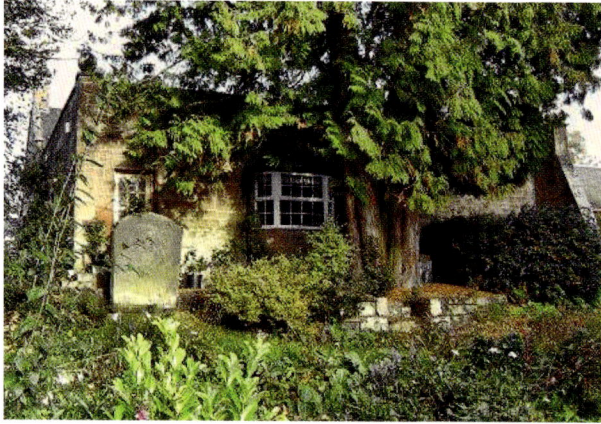

Sangguran Stone of 10th century known as the Minto Stone
Removed from Java and placed in the garden at Roxburghshire

Hindoo Pagoda below Barrackpore
© Trustees of the Victoria Memorial Hall, Calcutta

friendship by sending a black leopard trapped in the Eastern districts as a gift for the Barrackpore menagerie. Thus, Wellesley's menagerie continued to flourish in Minto's time.

Two important Javanese stone inscriptions of 10th century antiquity were removed from the Malang region and shipped to Calcutta in 1813 as a gift from Raffles to his patron Lord Minto. One of the stones was taken home by Minto to Scotland and placed at his ancestral seat in Roxburghshire in the Scottish borderlands. It is known as the Minto Stone and is present even today in the garden. The other stone is languishing in the godown of the Indian Museum in Calcutta.

Minto sets the tone for Barrackpore as a kind of Arcadia, a haven away from the ostentations and

View From Barrackpore
© British Library Board

machinations of city life. With its gardens and cottages, it offered a paradigm of paradise and served as a focal point for nostalgia and a vision of rural England. The scene offered grace and tranquillity, so much so that even the locals gained a shared beauty. In a moment of racial admiration, rare for the British, Minto describes the sepoys thus: 'The men themselves are still more ornamental. I never saw so handsome a race. They are much superior to the Madras people, whose forms I admired also. Those were slender; these are tall, muscular, athletic figures, perfectly shaped, and with the finest possible cast of countenance and features.'[9]

Again and again Minto refers to Barrackpore as a shelter from the vagaries of political life. 'I continue to enjoy Barrackpore and to find in it a real consolation. My Life would be comfortless without it. I hardly ever go out at Calcutta. . .. All that is to be done with people belongs to Calcutta. At Barrackpore I may read my dispatches in peace.'[10]

While his son John went jackal-hunting with friends, the father took a walk at sunset to catch the breeze along the riverside. In his letters home, Lord Minto continuously describes the pleasures of Barrackpore, ending with a lament on how during his evening walks he felt even more acutely the lack of a family life. He missed a wife by his side 'to tell how I like the breeze and the moon and the planets and such pretty prattle.'[11] Sometimes there were diversions in the form of a small dinner party or a *nautch* at a tent, lit by torches cast in hollow bamboo, with oil being poured on every now and then by the snuffers, 'men, black but handsome, and almost as naked as bronze figures which serve for candlesticks usually are.'[12] The *nautch* girls were pretty Cashmerian girls reminding him momentarily of 'Etruscan figures or those found at Pompey.'[13] Their

intoxication stole upon him as he sat by the light of the torches in a ring, an exotic entertainment with the eroticized figures of swaying lean bodies, and all at once the pull of the East whispered strong.

In the days following the Sepoy Revolt when race lines were to be strongly demarcated, such active and admiring participation in Indian pastimes was to be frowned upon. In Minto's time however it was allowable and more so because the Governor General had a genuine spirit of tolerance for the 'natives'.

It was also in his time that there was a collision of interests between the Serampore missionaries led by William Carey and the Court of Directors in England. The government in England was desirous of maintaining religious peace in India through a policy of non-interference and Lord Minto had

Une Nautch, 1832
Alexandre-Marie Colin
© Rogers Fund 1970
Metropolitan Musuem, New York

Designs for the Cenotaph at Barrackpore for Lord Minto
Front elevation (Scheme A), 1807
© RIBA Collections

The Cenotaph at Barrackpore, 2018
© Nikhil Kapur

The Cenotaph
© British Library Board

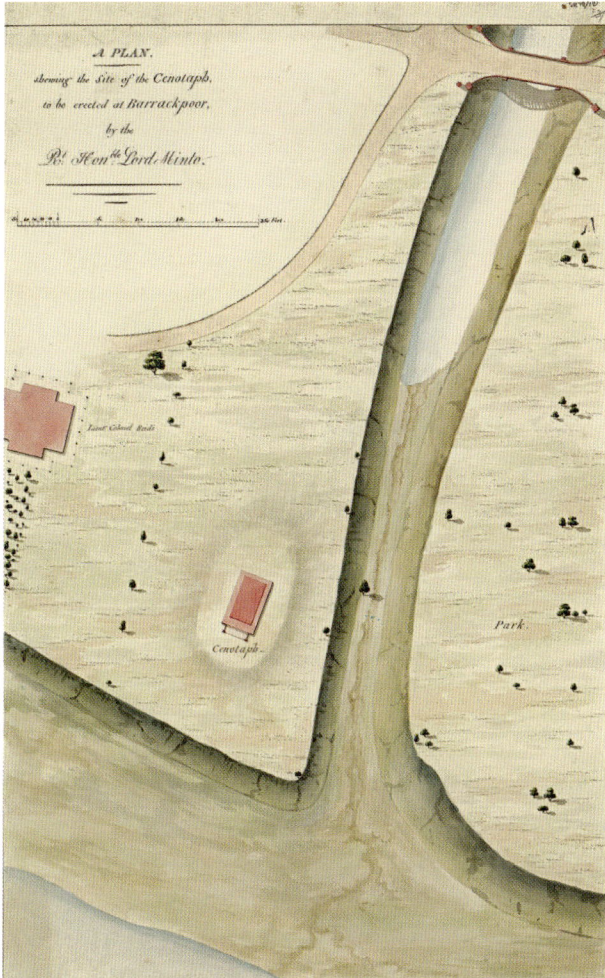

Site Plan for the Cenotaph at Barrackpore, 1810
George Rodney Blane
© RIBA Collections

Unknown Person on the Steps of the Cenotaph
© Raj Bhavan Archives Calcutta

prohibited public preaching and publications that might cause offence to Hindus or Muslims. A meeting was held at Barrackpore between Lord Minto, Carey and Marshman, where Minto—in a gesture of friendship—promised to let the English Press at Serampore continue. In 1808 however, in a private letter, he admitted that the writings of the Serampore Press were decidedly inflammatory. 'Pray read, especially, the miserable stuff addressed to the Gentoos, in which, without one word to convince or to satisfy . . . the pages are filled with hellfire, and hellfire, and still hotter fire...'[14] Once Serampore passed to British hands, they were careful to leave the missionaries alone and neither help nor hinder them in their work. As with everything else, moderation was the watchword in this policy. Lord Minto is known in history for his expeditions to Mauritius and Java. The expedition was a success but lives were lost, as is inevitable in the glories of war. With Barrackpore serving as a country retreat

William Carey
© Wikimedia commons

Joshua Marshman
© baptisthistory.com

William Ward
© Wikimedia commons

Minto used its grounds to create a fitting memorial. The cenotaph or the Temple of Fame, erected by him in 1813 as a memorial to those who had fallen in the Mauritius and Java campaigns of 1810-11 was built here and endures till today in classical perfection. The Memorial stands as a vindication of lives lost in the course of Empire, for the Java campaign would have been impossible without the Bengal and Madras troops who actually filled in for almost two - thirds of the British army.

Significantly, perhaps, mutinous feelings had already begun to stir in the Bengal regiments. In 1815, Bengal soldiers in Java who had begun to be increasingly aware of their shared Hindu past through the temples of Borobudur, planned to kill their British officers and establish a sepoy administration. The conspiracy was uncovered and 17 of the conspirators were shot by a firing squad.[15] But the grudge of the sepoys would remain and

burst out into flames again, ten years later, at Barrackpore.

After the campaigns overseas there was a new restlessness in Lord Minto to return home. Both his sons had taken wives in India and had been installed in Government House, Calcutta — where Minto found happiness in the semblance of a family with his sons and daughters-in-law. But the desire to go home was strong. 'So Molly, put the kettle on and I'll be with you in a trice',[16] he had written to his wife in 1810.

Barrackpore Park now mirrored this longing for England. 'This Barrackpore is a most happy change of scene from Batavia, and is indeed to me a kind of little Minto having a faint smack of some virtue in it.'[17] Hankering for home, it was still a year before orders from England came, coinciding with his own letters pleading for relief. In Barrackpore he had ominous dreams of being back home. 'I thought we were all walking on the Haugh.'[18]

His health was breaking down and in 1812 he complained of a dreadful feeling of lethargy. At last he was recalled in 1813 and set sail for England. He reached England in May, 1814, accompanied by his son Captain George Elliot, his younger son John and the wives and children of both his sons. He wrote to Lady Minto: 'Yesterday was indeed one of the happiest days of my life; but there is one happier still in store, when I shall have you once more in my arms.'[19]

In one of the most poignant blows of fate, Lord Minto caught a chill in the cold drizzling rain while attending the funeral of William Eden, 1st Baron Auckland, his brother-in-law and the father of the future Governor General. He died on 21st June in Stevenage, hours before reaching his beloved estate. Years later the letters written by Lady Minto to her husband in India were found tied together with a black string and inscribed 'Poor Fools'.

In Barrackpore, Lord Minto lives on in the architectural magnificence of the Cenotaph he had built in memory of those who had died in the expedition to Java. This cenotaph commemorates Lord Minto even today and is one with the other monuments in Barrackpore Park that speak of days long gone.

NOTES ───────────────────────────────

1. Minto, The Countess of. 1880. Lord Minto in India: Life and Letters of Gilbert Elliot First Earl of Minto from 1807-1814. Longmans, Green and Company.
2. Ibid.
3. Ibid.
4. Ibid.
5. Ibid.
6. Ibid.
7. Ibid.
8. Ibid.
9. Ibid.
10. Ibid.
11. Ibid.
12. Ibid.
13. Ibid.
14. Ibid.
15. Carey, Peter. 1977. 'The Sepoy conspiracy of 1815 in Java.' Bijdragen tot de Taal, Land en Volkenkunde 133. KITLV Press.
16. Minto, The Countess of.
17. Ibid.
18. Ibid.
19. Ibid.

CHAPTER THREE

THE AGRA FOUNTAIN

*"At Barrackpore, preparing for a short excursion above
Kishnagur. Our elephants and horses were
yesterday despatched to be in
readiness on our arrival"*

The Private Journal of the Marquess of Hastings
Governor-General and Commander-in-Chief in India
edited by the Marchioness of Bute

Lord Minto was succeeded by the Marquess of Hastings. Apart from being historically important as consolidating British might against the Marathas, Pindaris and the Gurkhas with his policy of expansion, he also has the distinction of having three roads in Calcutta named after him. During his lifetime his titles changed a number of times. He was born Francis Rawdon and was known as Lord Rawdon during his campaigns in the American War of Independence. In 1790 his uncle Francis Hastings died and he assumed the hyphenated title of Rawdon-Hastings. On the death of his father in 1793 he succeeded him as the second earl of Moira. In 1816 he was created the Marquess of Hastings as a reward for his successes against the Gurkhas with the subsidiary title of Viscount Loudon. Following the unfortunate practice of changing road names as a means of wiping out colonial history which dominated Calcutta a century and a half later, the names of Moira Street, Rawdon Street and Loudon Street were unimaginatively replaced, without taking into account the fact that the Marquess of Hastings is credited, in a large measure, with Calcutta's early town planning including the addition of new roads under the Lottery Committee and an all-important embankment along the river. This would evolve into the Strand Road, well praised by travellers like

Francis Rawdon-Hasting, 1789
Sir Joshua Reynolds
© Royal Collection, Windsor

palace on fair Hoogly's stream'[2] that is described so eloquently in a contemporary poem entitled *Tom Raw the Griffin*. Tom Raw describes the house as providing moments of solace to Hastings as he rested from the arduous task of Company governance;

'Twas here, from wars returning, Hastings spent,
His happiest Indian days, amidst the smiles
Of wedded love and infant blandishment
And friendship that made light his anxious toils.'[3]

Lord Hastings was a brisk man of business and though he kept a journal, he had little time to describe the beauties of Barrackpore, unlike his predecessor. We get glimpses of his life at the Park, however, readying elephants and horses for the long march up the country. On the same day a puppet show was set up for the amusement of his family where the figures were moved with much dexterity, though the Governor General wrote in his journal disparagingly about the entertainment; the figures were disproportionate to actual size and the monotony of the scenes was distressing. He also described an acrobatic performance of a man throwing himself through hoops held for his visitors and family. Puppet shows, acrobatics, magic shows and the like were favoured by sahibs till the end of colonial rule in India. Indeed the magician cum acrobat became a mysterious figure of the East and passed into English popular imagination, to be reborn later in the novels of Wilkie Collins and the stories of Sherlock Holmes.

Fanny Parks - 'a fine broad road has since been made along the side of the river, about two miles in length; it is a delightful drive in the evening, close to the ships.'[1]

Fittingly it was Hastings' endeavours that gave finality and shape to Government House, Barrackpore in the form by which it is visible today. The ruins of Wellesley's projected castle were pulled down. The temporary mansion built by Wellesley became the Government House. It was this 'regal

Moving in camp was a requisite for British administrators in India. One had to inspect possessions and territories, meet rulers and other notables and subtly communicate British might. In the case of Lord Hastings, he had also to keep

Governor General's House at Barrackpore
Sita Ram
© British Library Board

a close eye on the war in Nepal, then in progress. Hastings' journey was from Calcutta to the Punjab and back. Embarking in June 1814 on the *Soonamookie*, the Governor General's barge which set sail from Barrackpore, a convoy of 220 boats carried Lord and Lady Hastings, their children, secretaries, A.D.Cs, sepoys, food, stores and even palanquins. The elaborate flotilla of *Soonamookie* and *Feel-cherry* wound upstream while all along a posse of anxious zamindars presented him with *nuzzurs*. These included 'money, live partridges, deer, hares, and a porcupine.'[4] The animals were accepted for the Barrackpore menagerie but the money was accepted in token only and then declined as Hastings was fastidious in recording his well bred

honesty. The boats passed Nabadwip and then on to Murshidabad, Rajmahal, Patna, Benaras and Allahabad and to Cawnpore. From there the company marched on land till they reached Delhi.

In a fortuitous resurrection of forgotten texts, Hastings' private papers were rediscovered in Mount Stuart, the house of the Bute family in Scotland and acquired by the British Library in 1995. These papers included his journal, published in 1858 and edited by his daughter Lady Sophia. It is from this journal that his life in Barrackpore can be pieced together. It is a pity that Hastings grew 'too weary and too busy after 1818 to keep up the journal,'[5] or a more detailed account of his life in Calcutta and Barrackpore may have emerged. One of the greatest finds of the Hastings Collection is a set of eight albums of watercolours painted by the Indian artist Sita Ram. Details of the artist's identity are still sketchy. A portrait done of him in 1820 has been dissected by historians to provide clues to his persona. The portrait shows an elderly man dressed in an upper-class manner working in a quiet room in a mansion by a river which has been identified as a room in Barrackpore. Sita Ram was a painter probably trained in the Murshidabad School of Painting, before moving onto the Company Style which is described by art historians as creating watercolours showing Indian subjects pitched with a Europeanising style. Two of Sita Ram's albums contain drawings of birds and animals that could only be found at Barrackpore. These are fascinating sketches with fine detailing and natural light and shade depicting ladybirds, butterflies, trees as well as menagerie animals like the ostrich and the cassowary.

Paintings by Sita Ram at Barrackpore
© British Library Board

The watercolour albums are a visual complement to the Marquess' journal and were probably commissioned to illustrate and thereby make the scenes and events of the journal more vivid. Sita Ram's valuable body of paintings, exhibiting scenes of the journey are a delight for historians and connoisseurs of art. The pictures include some of the earliest drawings of Barrackpore Park and the *Soonamookie*.

To Hastings and his journal must also be given the credit of creating a long-serving mystery with all the ingredients of a classic teaser, including sinister intent, diabolical execution and sloppy cover-up. The tale concerns a portion within the Agra Fort which Hastings visited in the course of his travels to North India. Inside the fort he toured the *zenana*

and sententiously mused on mutability and the inevitable passing of grandeur: 'In one of the courts, the pavement was inlaid with squares of black and white, to represent a chess board, so that the Emperor might make the female slaves perform the moves of that game between him and his Begums. Thus in this life we delude ourselves with costly and laborious preparations for amusements, in which we rarely if even once indulge ourselves when the arrangement is perfected.'6 Later he chanced upon the ruins of the *hammam* or bath of Shah Jahan - a suite of vaulted rooms within the *zenana*. The marble bath caught his fancy and he made yet another case for monumental glory, abandoned and derelict: 'Among the mounds of ruins in different parts I observed a number of large slabs, with much carving on them,

Bath Chambers at Agra Palace, 1815
Sita Ram
© British Library Board

lying neglected. I requested the magistrate to have them collected and sent down to Calcutta; prohibiting, however, the touching of any which might retain their places in walls, although the buildings might be otherwise in ruin.'[7]

In 1982, art historian Ebba Koch published an article entitled *The Lost Colonnade of Shah Jahan's Bath in the Red Fort of Agra* in which, using archival records as well as actual pieces of the column in the custody of the V&A Museum, she concluded that the dismantled pieces of colonnade had been shipped to England as spoils of the *hammam*: 'This bath represents today the only instance of a spoliated building in the otherwise remarkably well preserved (restored) ensemble of Shah Jahan's contribution to the Agra Fort.'[8]

Quoting from Colonel Sleeman she established how the Marquess of Hastings initiated or perhaps collaborated in this classic example of imperial plunder: 'The Marquess of Hastings, when Governor General of India (1813-32), broke up one of the most beautiful marble baths of this palace to send home to George IV of England, then Prince Regent, and the rest of the marble of the suite of apartments from which it has been taken, with all its exquisite fretwork and mosaic, was afterwards sold by auction, intent the task of preservation and restoration and removed a marble fountain from Agra, causing it to be sent to Calcutta: 'I consequently directed the marble of this chamber, as well as the white marble basin of a fountain which I found in the artillery-yard, full of all kinds of lumber, to be raised and shipped for Calcutta, where they may be somehow or other employed as ornaments to the city.'[10] Perhaps Hastings was conscious of his action as being an obvious act of plunder, for he recorded how the Collector and the Magistrate assured him that 'there were not ten persons in the city who knew of the existense of those baths and certainly not one who had the least notion of respecting them.'[11] The fate of the other pieces of marble is unknown. The marble bath was later traced by Curzon as being installed in Government House, Barrackpore.

At the time of writing this account the fountain, long buried in mud by the southern entrance to the house and somehow surviving seventy two years of neglect has been lovingly restored. Certainly Hastings' was not the first example of wrongful appropriation. The British habit of plundering national treasures had begun earlier and continued long after. Some of the plunder they took back with them, as was the case with Lord Minto, while other articles were used to decorate the palaces of the Raj as in the Viceregal Lodge, Simla, Government House, Calcutta or, as seen above, Government House, Barrackpore.

Moving in camp, travelling up the country and meeting most of the principal chieftains, rajas, zamindars and princes of the time added to British knowledge about the new lands they were slowly becoming masters of, as well as enabling them to exhibit themselves to the newly appropriated people.

Portrait of Sita Ram, by a Calcutta Artist, 1820
Private Collection London
© J. P. Losty
Picturesque Views of Hindustan

on account of our government, by the order of the then Governor General of India, Lord W. Bentinck...'[9] Fortunately, the auction fetched little; had it proved financially successful there might not have been much of the Taj left over for the world to enjoy!

In Volume 2 of his journal, Hastings referred to another day's visit to the Agra Fort where once again he was suitably moved by the majesty of its fallen grandeur. He approached with business-like

Paintings by Sita Ram at Barrackpore
© British Library Board

The fruits of these experiences were felt in Hastings' administrative reforms as well as in his attempts at consolidating Company rule. In renovating and adding to Government House Barrackpore, Hastings finished Wellesley's work. As such the house at Barrackpore was also a part of this process of strengthening and consolidation.

It is noteworthy that it was in his time, during the Gurkha Wars, that a tract of the Himalayas was leased to the British. It was in these parts of the Himalayas that the first hill settlements began which were later to grow into summer retreats for the British. The first house in Simla had been built by Captain Charles Kennedy in 1822 as the summer residence of the Commander-in-Chief of British India. The settlement was to grow into the town of Simla. From the middle of the 19th century, Simla would push Barrackpore into relative obscurity.

Paintings by Sita Ram at Barrackpore
© British Library Board

Wedding Procession of Lady Hastings' Cousin Jean Mary Campbell to James Munro Macnabb, Barrackpore Park, 1820
Sita Ram
© Macnabb Albums

NOTES

1. Parkes, Fanny. 2002. Begums, Thugs and White Mughals: The Journals of Fanny Parkes. Eland Publishing. Edited by William Dalrymple.

2. D'Oyly, Charles. 1828. Tom Raw, The Griffin: A Burlesque Poem, In Twelve Cantos: Illustrated By Twenty-Five Engravings, Descriptive Of The Adventures Of A Cadet In The East India Company's Service, From The Period of His Quitting England To His Obtaining A Staff Situation In India. R. Ackermann.

3. Ibid

4. Rawdon-Hastings, Francis. 1858. The Private Journal of the Marquess of Hastings. Saunders and Otley. Edited by The Marchioness of Bute.

5. Losty, J.P 2015. Picturesque Views of India, Sita Ram, Lord Hastings's Journey From Calcutta To The Punjab, 1814-15. Roli Books.

6. Rawdon-Hastings, Francis.

7. Ibid.

8. Koch, Ebba 1982. 'The Lost Colonnade of Shah Jahan's Bath in the Red Fort of Agra', The Burlington Magazine, Vol. 124, No. 951 (Jun., 1982).

9. Rawdon-Hastings, Francis.

10. Ibid.

11. Ibid.

CHAPTER FOUR

DISQUIET

> "Elephants, it appears, were not allowed in Calcutta
> or within five miles of it, but at Barracpur
> they were in order"

Lord Amherst and the British Advance Eastwards to Burma
Anne Thackeray Ritchie and Richardson Evans

Before Lord Wellesley arrived and clothed British rule in a stiff ceremonial formality, British life in Calcutta for the merchants and writers of the East India Company was one of riotous saturnalia. Relations between the Indians and the British were of mutual dependence. In the early 18th century, many English merchants were half-Indianised, with Indian wives or concubines, broods of half-Indian children and hybrid meals of soup, roast fowl, curry and rice with the pleasures of a *hookah* or a *nautch* afterwards. William Hickey's memoirs describe how British life in Calcutta included prodigious amounts of claret and Madeira, sweet-scented Persian tobacco dressed with sugar and spice bubbling through *hookahs* as its coils encircled the smokers' waists like snakes.

By the time Wellesley became Governor General, these frivolities had been replaced by an imperial aloofness. One of the needs of the British in India, as their territories grew, was to maintain a careful distancing by creating pockets of Englishness wherever possible. To this end, the clubs replaced the *nautches* of the earlier years. These clubs became the bastions of imperial rule with their bars, libraries, billiard-rooms, bridge-rooms, rattan chairs on verandahs and servants in cummerbunds strewn stiffly around. Similarly, the houses of the Anglo-Indians in India looked tropical from the outside with their gleaming walls of lime. Inside, however, the huge dining rooms, teak doors, marble floors, richly-carved fireplaces and English prints on the walls reminded one of an upper class mansion in

2 Middleton Street, North Side
Photographer Unknown
© The J. Paul Getty Museum, Los Angeles

2 Middleton Street, South View
Photographer Unknown
© The J. Paul Getty Museum, Los Angeles

England. Around these mansions stood ornamental lakes and landscaped gardens, also created along the lines of the English country house. The pull of their island-home remained strong and most British-built houses and gardens were attempts to recreate the lost scenes of youth.

Alongside the political, military and social history of the Anglo-Indian experience flowed an assertion of cultural practices through garden-making and plant experiences. The natural English love of gardening and botanical knowledge resulted in many experiments in fusion gardening. Gardens

Lady Teignmouth's Garden House on the Banks of the Hoogli [Calcutta], 1795
Hubert Cornish
© Caroline Simpson Library & Research Collection, Sydney Living Museums

Our Quarters in Calcutta
Artist Unknown
© Gift of Harry Friedman, 2005
Metropolitan Museum, New York

marked out European spaces and civil lines from native quarters through the careful cultivation of English flowers, fruits and European styled landscaping. Yet the vagaries of the tropical climate meant that many gardens also had to include Asian flora and fauna. Barrackpore Park bears witness to such a change.

To go back a little, even before Wellesley had created the pleasure gardens at Barrackpore, the British in Calcutta were absorbed in creating English style houses and gardens. Calcutta's villa houses along the Chowringhee and at Garden Reach were the opposite of Indian house designs. While the Indian elite lived in houses looking inward, built around a square courtyard, the British adapted European styles to the Indian climate and created Palladian houses with lofty verandahs, colonnaded fronts and a portico where the coach could draw up in shade. The house was usually in a compound and was surrounded by service quarters, lawns, flower beds and vegetable patches in as near an

approximation of the manor house style of England as could be achieved. Belvedere House in Alipore built in 1775 as Warren Hastings' garden house is a good example of this style.

Hastings in particular was an avid gardener and decorated his villas, both at Belvedere and at Hastings House with trees from all over Asia. His love of gardening matched his Spartan life—eating sparingly, bathing with cold water daily and retreating to bed by ten. These were oddities in comparison to the lifestyles of the other servants of the Company, who drifted around the countryside attending noisy revelries. From the time of his arrival in India, Hastings wrote to England for seeds of honeysuckle and sweet briar, for truffles, morels and artichokes which he tried to grow on Indian soil. On his return home to England, Hastings spent almost 60,000 pounds on his estate at Daylesford, constructing walks, lakes, waterfalls and a wooded road.

In 1786 the left bank of the Hooghly, opposite Calcutta, was the site of the Botanic Gardens founded by Alexander Kyd for encouraging scientific enquiry and commercial expediency, where rare trees were collected, grown, documented and precious produce like the tea bush were cultivated. The Company liked to think that the main function of the Botanic Gardens was commercial, but its directors hoped it would also be a scientific establishment for observing and classifying tropical plants. One could eventually also buy seeds and cuttings from it for one's private gardens.

By the time Wellesley had built the Government House at Calcutta and begun another at Barrackpore, Calcutta's urban landscape had shifted in emphasis from mercantile centre to imperial city.

Natural history drawings from the Francis Buchanan Collection Calcutta, done at Barrackpore
© Asiatic Society Calcutta

The horticultural project at Barrackpore was not just laying out a park but part of the wider discourse of imperial identity. Homesick and yet having to work and stay in India for the power and the pelf, Wellesley and his successors transplanted English gardens onto Indian soil to make a temporary existence seem more secure.

Barrackpore was part-residence, part-pleasure garden and was described as Wellesley's second palace, with pretty grounds upon which he erected a riding house, a fine aviary and a well-stocked menagerie. The last named, like the Botanic Gardens, was part of the English desire to acquire and understand foreign species at a time when British naturalists of the 18th and 19th centuries found the study of remote organisms very exciting. These collections enhanced the whole culture of imperial enterprise because they were seen as important knowledge-banks for animals and plants which could aid government decisions regarding commerce and expansion. The Barrackpore menagerie was to have been part of the Natural History department of the Fort William College, which was envisioned by Wellesley to be an institution priming the new young factors with knowledge about the lands they were to rule.

In time Barrackpore Park gathered other accoutrements that made it a country residence fit for a Governor General. Lord Minto's Cenotaph was built along the lines of a Greek temple. The Marquess of Hastings brought in the Lotus Fountain, which fitted well with the Italianized landscape while Lady Loudon, his wife, constructed a greenhouse on the site of Wellesley's original and abandoned house. Lord Curzon later traces the greenhouse to be near the bandstand in the Park, below the landing stage or lower ghat.[1] Sarah, Countess of Amherst, whose husband William Pitt Amherst succeeded the Marquess of Hastings as Governor General, revelled in the exotic plants at Barrackpore and is said to have strolled through the garden with Nathaniel Wallich, head of the Calcutta Botanical Gardens, as her guide. In her words, 'I find new flowers, the names, properties, and culture of which I know nothing till Dr. Wallich inform'd me upon all these points.'[2] At Barrackpore, noted the traveller Fanny Parks approvingly in 1824, 'during the races the Calcutta

Banyan Tree, Calcutta, 1860s
© Gift of Matthew Dontzin, 1985
Metropolitan Museum, New York

Redcliffe Hotel from Paignton Beach
The house was the former residence of Colonel Robert Smith
who used his architectural experiences in India
to develop his style, which fuses Indian and Gothic elements

Nathaniel Wallich

Lord Amherst

world assembles there, we went over for a week; it was delightful to be again in the country. Lady Amherst rendered the Government House gay with quadrilles and displays of fireworks...'[3] But there was always the presence of the Company, snapping at their heels with the old dictum of thrift and Parks wondered whether his Lordship's intention of planting potatoes in the Park at Barrackpore is serious because 'all this European economy produces considerable surprise.'[4]

Perhaps the Amhersts, left to themselves, would have done more. Lord Amherst was certainly well travelled enough to be an amateur botanist himself. In 1816 he had been sent as ambassador to Canton to persuade the Chinese officials there to legalize the British factory. Amherst returned a year later to England having travelled as far down as Batavia, Rio de Janeiro, and even St Helena where he had met Napoleon.

In 1823 Amherst arrived in India with his wife Sarah, Countess of Amherst, his son Jeff and his daughter Sarah. Lady Amherst's *Journal* contains vivid accounts of her life in India. The *Journal* records lively accounts of typically Indian experiences which fill Anglo-Indian narratives-of sati, cholera, native female schools, Hindu festivals, Burmese princesses and so on. Lady Amherst notes how their daily round of tedium in Calcutta was interrupted by short tours exploring the town and the country escorted by aides-de-camp. They camped under trees and were delighted to find troupes of admiring and friendly villagers coming forward with bananas, vegetables and even tumblers of milk. In 1825, Simla had not yet been built up as a retreat and the Governor General and his Ladyship had to make do with the plains. The journal describes health excursions up the river on the *Soonamookie* with pinnaces, baggage boats and budgerows in tow, a noisy camp of five hundred men who travelled up to Murshidabad and met the Resident.

Such times of peaceful enjoyment were however not long to last. In 1824 Barrackpore recorded its first ominous signs of dissent in a revolt by sepoys at the cantonment. The sepoys' disaffection began with the long campaigns in Burma and the Arakan expedition to which they were being sent. Tired after a long march from Mathura to Barrackpore, they were now ordered to trek a distance of 800 kilometers to Chittagong in preparation for the campaign. The arduous trek was resented by the sepoys for the difficult terrain as well as the long and grim march, made further difficult by their meagre pay. They had to provide for their carriage out of their own allowances, and since carriage included ammunition and muskets as well as cooking pots and other daily necessities, this was looked upon with disfavour. There was no question of using the more advantageous sea route as that meant crossing the forbidden waters which was still taboo. Cattle, normally used as beasts of burden by the sepoys, had been so much in demand by the Company officials in the sea-borne expedition to Rangoon that there were few left for the sepoys. The sepoys demanded either carriage bullocks or an enhanced payment of double *batta* or allowances.

On the 1st of November the 47th regiment was asked to commence the march followed by the 26th regiment and 62nd regiment. The soldiers of the

Barrackpore House [Calcutta] around 1819
James Prinsep
© Caroline Simpson Library & Research Collection, Sydney Living Museums

Photographs of the Bindee Baba Temple, Barrackpore
The temple came up adjacent to the tree from where sepoy Bindee Tewaree was hanged
© Soumen Mitra, 2019

47th refused to bring their knapsacks at the parade ground of the Barrackpore Cantonment, still arguing over their demands. The commanding officer General Dalzell was unable to impose his orders and went to Calcutta to consult with the Commander-in-Chief General Edward Paget. The sepoys under the leadership of Bindee Tiwaree refused to leave the parade ground. Here is what happened next according to Lady Amherst: 'Early on the morning of the 1st General Dalzell went up to the Commander-in-chief and before three o' clock that day, himself and all his staff arrived at Barrackpur. Soon after, the bodyguard consisting of 300 men went up in a boat to overtake General Cotton's regiment. It had proceeded 30 miles up the river but arrived here, as did the Royals from Calcutta, by 11 at night. Some artillery also arrived from Dumdum; the house was therefore well guarded on all sides and all the avenues to it and we then thought ourselves safe...by daybreak on November 1, Sir E. Paget, who had with his staff bivouacked in the greenhouse put himself at the head of the troops. The canon from Dumdum was stationed in the Park to fire over the pales on the insurgents if necessary.'[5] Lady Amherst, along with her daughter Sarah, who was ill, waited stoically in Government House as a terrible battle broke out between the British commanders and the Indian

Edward Paget

Subedar of 21st Bengal Native Infantry

Doorgah Preparations Opposite to Isherah
William Prinsep, 1832
© Caroline Simpson Library & Research Collection,
Sydney Living Museums

Ghat near Barrackpore
William Prinsep, 1832
© Caroline Simpson Library & Research Collection,
Sydney Living Museums

My House at Garden Reach Calcutta
William Prinsep, 1837
© Caroline Simpson Library & Research Collection,
Sydney Living Museums

sepoys, what Lady Amherst describes as 'English soldiers firing on British uniforms.'[6] Shots entered the cookhouse, sepoys fell into the water in their effort to swim the Ganges to safety and soon the river was filled with corpses of dead sepoys. The following day twelve of the mutineers were hanged in chains in front of the lines while their bodies were later thrown into the river. The leader Bindee Tiwaree was apprehended in disguise in the Lines four days later and was hanged, following which his body was suspended in chains on an adjacent gibbet as a macabre exhibition of British triumph. The Bindee Baba temple still stands on the site where the leader Bindee Tiwaree was hanged.

Though a free pardon was later granted to the rest of the regiment and their death sentence commuted to hard labour, Lady Amherst notes how the pardon was received with apathy and the prisoners 'asked for their copper pots and marched home – a most disappointing result indeed.'[7]

In spite of Lady Amherst's shrill justifications in the rest of her journal concerning her husband's role, contemporary reaction was critical of the Governor General. Amherst was mocked as an 'evil genius' by *The Oriental Herald* of May 1825, published in London, which described the incident some time later as the '*Barrackpore Massacre*'. It criticized Paget for his indiscriminate slaughter of what was after all a peaceful protest for enhanced pay and provisions. Many sepoys deserted the British army after the incident and a Court of Enquiry set up after the event felt the grievances justifiable. Though Lord Amherst was almost recalled for his irresponsible role in not being able to control the excesses of the Army commander, he managed to stay on till 1828. But only just.

Lord Willam Bentinck
A Portrait by Sir Thomas Lawrence

which had been sinking for the past twelve hours stopped...had it pleased God to have spared his life till the 29th, he would have completed his twenty-fourth year. On August 3rd at break of day our dearly beloved son was interred in the burial-ground at Barrackpore with military honours.'[8]

Fanny Parks mourned the death of Jeffrey Amherst as the passing of yet another Englishman in India: 'A gloom has been thrown over Calcutta; and Lord Amherst's family are in the deepest affliction, caused by the death of Captain Amherst which took place a short time ago. His lordship, his son, and his nephew were seized with fever at the same time; Captain Amherst's became typhus, and carried him off.'[9]

In 1827 the Amherst family arrived in Simla and the first of the great Simla anecdotes is recorded. On 10th April Lady Amherst records her first impressions: 'Large flocks of sheep laden with merchandise come over these nearly inaccessible mountains...we spend our time most monotonously rising early and walking, or rather scrambling up the mountains. After breakfast, go out with the native botanist in search of new plants. Our morning home occupations ensue till 5 in the evening, when we sally forth among the mountains; dine at 7, and retire to rest at 9 o' clock.'[10] Lord Amherst was the first Governor General who made Simla his place of retreat from the plains. The fashion was continued by his successors.

Amherst was followed by Lord Bentinck who is celebrated in history for his social reforms and impetus to Western education but in the context of Barrackpore cuts a lack-lustre figure. The indomitable Fanny Parkes notes diapprovingly that 'Lord William has been doing away with all the

Fate continued to be cruel to the Amhersts. Even as they had got over the shock of the Revolt, and what was to them the very unjustified censure of Lord Amherst, came a fresh blow. Their son Jeffrey who had come out to India with his parents died at Barrackpore and was buried in the military cemetery. In July 1826 Lady Amherst's journal records how the boy, seemingly recovering, suddenly had a violent relapse of the fever. 'We had all gone on board his pinnace and sat an hour or two with him at Barrackpur. Not long after we landed I received two notes from him, pressing me to send him medicine as his fever was coming on again. We got him ashore as soon as possible, violently and dangerously ill, which illness continued with little or no intermission until a quarter past nine in the morning of August the 2nd, when his pulse good appointments in the Civil Service; and the army have been cruelly treated in, with respect to the half-batta.'[11]

Calcutta society was aghast at his prudish dealings and another traveller, Emma Roberts, deplored the parsimonious habits of the 'present government' which 'gave away birds and beasts without remorse'[12] instead of increasing the exhibits and sending them to England for zoological societies. Apart from closing down the aviary there seems to have been not much use for Barrackpore in Bentinck's times, though the Honeymoon Lodge - one of the bungalows used frequently by newly marrieds as the Governor General's guest house was frequently let to couples for short periods.

By the time Lord Ellenborough arrived in 1842 after the tenure of Lord Auckland the house was important and scenic enough for him to land there first and thence proceed to Calcutta. 'His lordship arrived at Barrackpore on the afternoon of Wednesday the 12th of July, and on the 13th, went to Calcutta, where he took his seat in council... Shortly after his lordship's arrival at Barrackpore the military of that station gave him a ball and supper at which some hundreds of people were present. After supper the speeches were highly complimentary; his lordship was very full of his regard for the army, and also stated his intention to reside quietly at Barrackpore, as a country-gentleman; visiting Government House at Calcutta merely on council days, for a few hours twice a week.'[13]

Lord Ellenborough added a broad terrace walk that ran around the old river bank from the lower landing stage to the house. The house had thus a lived-in air and was proper enough to be enjoyed as the weekend retreat in the English gentry tradition. The gardens and house were structured to mimic as closely as possible the characteristics of an English rural retreat. But such Englishness was after all a pretence, for beyond the house stood India in full force, with its temples dedicated to 'Hanumanji' or the 'Monkey God', its burning ghats, its villages and jungle and the broad river beyond, on which bobbed boats, barges and the occasional corpse. Barrackpore represented a slice of English life against an otherwise unfamiliar and disquieting background of India.

Sezincote House

Chimney piece with figures of Hindu ladies carrying Ganges water at Warren Hastings' villa at Daylesford

We end with a paradox. While the Governors General were anxiously parading Englishness in Barrackpore, a group of ex-India Englishmen who had lived and worked in India carried the imprint of their Indian lives back home.

Somewhere in England, in the Cotswolds, Warren Hastings had created a villa at Daylesford, near Adlestrop, using Indian design templates complete with onion dome. The house was built by Samuel Pepys Cockerell, architect to the East India Company. Hasting's house was neo-classical with a large number of Indian features including a dome and Indian figures carved around the fireplace. Samuel Cockerell took the Indian motifs further

in a house built for his brother, Colonel Cockerell, who was another *nabob*. This house was named Sezincote and was built on the Saracenic pattern, with rounded domes, crouching Nandi bulls and a temple of Souriya. Here, in 'a piece of Deccan in the Cotswold,'[14] is yet another variation of the Anglo-Indian dream.

Later Colonel Robert Smith of the East India Company built Redcliffe House in Devon, also using a mixture of Indian and Italian styles. Smith had been a successful surveyor for the East India Company and in this task had travelled far and wide in Company's lands and had survived the wilds of India for many years in the mid 19th

Semaphore Tower of Barrackpore with Flagstaff Bungalow
Colonel Robert Smith
© British Library Board

century. He also restored the major monuments of Delhi and developed his taste in experimental fusion style architecture. Besides this, he sketched and painted many hundreds of British troop movements and Company life alongside views of Indian temples, monuments and landscapes. One of these is a painting of Barrackpore cantonment and the Government House.

Thus, while Barrackpore Park was a corner of a foreign field true to England, India itself took pride of place in some of the buildings back home. Colonialism shaped forms of government and institutions in colonised nations while at the same time influencing English identity and history. The imperial imaginaries and projects thus reformulated British thought also.

In the mingling of two very different cultures using the garden and building as a space of contestation, interesting variations were made which are visible even today.

NOTES

1. K.G, The Marquis Curzon of Kedleston. 1925. British Government in India: The Story of the Viceroys and Government Houses. Cassel and Company Ltd.
2. Thackeray-Ritchie, Anne and Evans, Richardson. 1909. Lord Amherst and the British Advance Eastwards Through Burma. University of Oxford.
3. Parkes, Fanny. 2002. Begums, Thugs and White Mughals: The Journals of Fanny Parkes. Eland Publishing. Edited by William Dalrymple.
4. Ibid.
5. Thackeray-Ritchie, Anne and Evans, Richardson.
6. Ibid.
7. Ibid.
8. Ibid.
9. Parkes, Fanny.
10. Thackeray-Ritchie, Anne and Evans, Richardson.
11. Parkes, Fanny.
12. Roberts, Emma. 1837. Scenes and Characteristics of Hindostan, With Sketches of Anglo-Indian Society. W.H. Allen and Co.
13. Anonymous. 1842. The British Friend of India Magazine and Indian Review. Vol II, August-January. Smith, Elder and Co, Cornhill.
14. Malins, Edward. 1980. 'Indian Influences on English houses and gardens at the beginning of the Nineteenth Century', Garden History Vol 8 No 1. The Garden History Society.

CHAPTER FIVE

A REALLY PRETTY PLACE

❝

"Yes! this is certainly the place to live at. George must find out that he can Governor-General here, as well as at Calcutta."

Letters from India by the Hon.E.E
Ed The Hon. Eleanor Eden

❞

Lord Auckland arrived in India in 1836 when, Government House, Barrackpore had assumed its final shape. The Governors General and their families who lived in it had brought to it attitudes of resentment, tolerance or love based on their personal histories.

Possibly the most complicated response was that of Emily and Fanny Eden, the sisters of Lord Auckland who was a bachelor and had been accompanied by them on his Indian sojourn. The Eden letters are copious, especially the ones written by Emily Eden and have been published at various times by members of their family. Three volumes are out till date: *Letters from India* edited by her niece Eleanor Eden (1871), *Up the Country* — an account of her journey to the Upper Provinces (1866) and *Miss Eden's Letters*, edited by her great-niece Violet Dickinson (1919). Prophetic in her introduction to *Up the Country*, Emily Eden mourned the passing of an era when life was slower, more picturesque and possibly more exotically alluring: 'Now that India has fallen under the curse of railroads, and that life and property will soon become as insecure there as they are here, the splendour of a Governor General's progress is at an end. The Kootub will probably become a Railway Station; the Taj will, of course, under the sway of an Agra Company (Limited, except for destruction) be bought up for a monster hotel; and the Governor General will dwindle down into a first-class passenger with a carpet bag.'[1]

George Eden, 1st Earl of Auckland, 1850
© National Portrait Gallery, London

Had Miss Eden known that about two decades later a new western-educated Indian middle class would be questioning their role in British India and the purpose of colonial rule as a whole, her remarks may not have been so airily bestowed. In 1866 all that Emily Eden was lamenting upon was the period of passive native obedience that had passed with the Revolt.

The British women who had come out to India were primarily wives of civilians or military officers, female servants, missionaries, a scattering of adventurous travellers and a few of the 'fishing fleet'- young women shipping themselves out to procure a suitable husband. Emily Eden did not match this standard demography of colonial personnel. She was too intellectually agile, too lively and brisk for the life of a languishing wife. She loved politics, the cerebral company of men and although Lord Melbourne, the Whig politician had expressed a matrimonial interest, Emily felt she was too different from standards of femininity to confirm herself into wifehood. In her letters about India and Barrackpore there is a wit that reminds one of the vivacity of Jane Austen's humour, certainly the two novels that Emily Eden wrote on her return to England have the charm of an English Manners comedy that remind us of Austen.

Above all Emily Eden was devoted to her brother George and 'thought of George and herself as a permanent couple, and she was quite as dutiful and caring in regards to his physical and mental wellbeing as any wife.'[2] It was thus taken for granted by even King William IV that the two sisters would accompany Lord Auckland to India when he was appointed as such in 1835. 'His majesty is not surprised that Miss Eden and her Sister should have determined to accompany so affectionate a Brother even to so remote a destination, and He is sensible how much their Society must contribute to his comfort.'[3] And so, towards the end of September 1835 Lord Auckland, his two sisters, their nephew William Godolphin Osborne, six servants and Chance the spaniel set off for India. For six years Emily maintained a copious correspondence with family and friends in Europe and managed to include comments on everything she engaged with.

In England Emily's daily routine had included writing letters, sketching, reading, social visits and

Emily Eden and Chance the spaniel, 1835
Simon Jacques Rochard
© National Portrait Gallery, London

gardening. The last had been a great activity since it involved close camaraderie with George. It was in the garden at her beloved house in Greenwich that she received news of George Auckland's promotion as First Lord of the Admiralty, the first in a sweeping career change. Gone were the days of laughter and gossip and glorious gardening: 'Our glorious promotion was inflicted on us on a particular Thursday...which George and I had set apart for a holiday...There I sat under the verandah crying. What else could be done, with the roses all out, and the sweet peas and the whole garden looking perfectly lovely.'[4]

The Eden sisters were lively, witty and often biting in their accounts. While Fanny Eden had a more

adventurous attitude towards India, Emily deplored their stay. They had come, as she confided in a letter, simply for the money. 'If we live to come home, we shall be very much better off than we could ever have expected to be, for there is no doubt that the Governor General's place is well-paid.'[5]

Ironically though it is in the Eden sisters' accounts that we experience the thrill of discovering India in a much more realistic manner than any that had been written till now. Their seven years' sojourn in India, captured in their letters and journals, catches a sense of the actual country rather than the romanticized Orientalism of letters and accounts written later in the 19th century.

The Eden sisters came to India at a time when Indian rulers still commanded respect. The titular Mughal emperor, though shrunk in power, was regarded by many as the rightful ruler of India. He maintained court ceremony, including Urdu poetry contests and had a posse of Imperial elephants strolling down the Chandni Chowk. In Punjab, Ranjit Singh was still alive and though old, was presented as someone formidable and a match for the British. For Lady Amherst Ranjit Singh had been a troublesome and fearful person - 'a ghastly figure and when mounted upon his high-bred steed his phantom face and bird-like limbs, his long hoary beard and withered form, pictured death on a pale horse.'[6] For Emily Eden, there was affection and something almost touching respect in her description of the old king. 'Old Runjeet looks much more personable on horseback than in durbar and is so animated on all military matters that he rides about with the greatest activity... Still he has made himself a great King; he has conquered a great many powerful enemies; he is remarkably just

Dost Muhammad Khan
Sketch by Emily Eden
© British Library Board

Ranjit Singh
Sketch by Emily Eden
© Trustees of the Victoria Memorial Hall, Calcutta

in his government; he has disciplined a large army; he hardly ever takes away life which is wonderful in a despot; and he is excessively loved by his people.'[7]

In her travels throughout India Emily wavered between a haughty condescension and a bright interest in her surroundings. The doings and beings of the strange land kept her fascinated. There was never the air of proud isolation that marked British awareness after 1857. Emily Eden sketched Ranjit Singh, went to a party given by him at the Shalimar Gardens, petted his grandchildren and conversed with his wives. She wrote of the Raja of Benaras and all the other Indian chiefs she met with respect and admiration. After the Revolt, these real men were to be replaced by cardboard Maharajahs and Nawabs who nodded and bobbed to the Queen's representatives. The representatives themselves were no longer sent out by the Company, but were professionally-managed civil servants or 'Competition-wallahs'—those who had come out through a competitive examination. For the Eden sisters, however, India was real in its princes and jewellery, its elephants and howdahs, its *Emaunburra* and the *Rooma Durwanee* in Lucknow. Sometimes it was as

Durbar of Lord Auckland
Sketch by Emily Eden
© Indoislamica

if India had taken a hold on Emily and she could feel the ruinous effect of colonialism. In a poignant aside, writing of her meeting with the Mughal Emperor in Delhi, Emily Eden even feels his sadness, sitting in the garden with a *chowrybadar* waving the flies from him 'and somehow I feel that we horrid English have just gone and done it, merchandised it, revenued it and spoiled it all.'[8]

During her stay in India, Emily tried to continue the routine of English life, including sketching and gardening. But the heat and dust of India seemed to have sapped and weakened her more than her sister Fanny. Fanny Eden succumbed to the novelties of life in India, went tiger hunting in Rajmahal and dashed off to Murshidabad from where she returned 'quite brushed up by her expedition, and has not suffered half so much as I should have expected from the heat of the last week... '[9] Emily Eden's letters touch on the heat and her discomfort repeatedly: 'But then that horrid old wretch the sun comes ranting up; the tents get baked through; and all through the camp there is a general moulting of fur shoes and merino and shawls, then an outcry for muslin and then for a Punkah to give us breath.'[10] In November 1839 she writes to say that 'the heat is quite dreadful, and I think I feel my brain simmering up in small bubbles, just as water does before it is beginning to boil.'[11] And in March she begins a letter with the full force of her

Sketch by Emily Eden
© Trustees of the Victoria Memorial Hall, Calcutta

annoyance: 'Got up with half a headache for want of sleep; the Brahminee kites and the crows and the pariah dogs all croaked and cawed and howled all night.'[12]

Nor are all her remarks on Indians charitable! 'Then as to the Hindu College the boys are educated, as you say, by the Government, at least under its active patronage, and they are British subjects inasmuch as Britain has taken India, and in many respects they may be called well-educated young men; but still I cannot tell you what the wide difference is between a European and a Native. An elephant and Chance, St Paul's and a Baby-Home...a diamond and bad flint... I do not see how the prejudices ever can wear out, nor do I see that it is very desirable.'[13] As she got to know India better through camp-life, the querulous tone is beaten down sometimes by a lively interest in the Indian princes. The letters and entries related to Ranjit Singh are as free from racial slant as possible.

It thus comes as a relief to know that the one enjoyable aspect of life in India when not in camp was Barrackpore. From the start Emily envisioned Government House as a relief from the very public and thereby distasteful life at Calcutta. 'I have described our Calcutta house and household so often that I cannot do it again. It is all very magnificent, but I cannot endure our life there. We go there on Monday morning before breakfast. We have great dinners of 50 people, fathers and mothers unknown, to say nothing of themselves. Every Monday and Wednesday evening Fanny and I are at home to anybody who is on what is called the Government House list...on Thursday morning we also receive any people who chance to notify themselves the day before. . .'[14]

And so Barrackpore provided a refuge from enforced socializing and living the part of a Lady Sahib. 'On Thursday afternoon we always come here (Barrackpore) and a prodigious pleasure it is. It feels something like home. It is sixteen miles from Calcutta, on the river-side. A beautiful fresh green park, a lovely flower garden, a menagerie that has been neglected; but there is a foundation of a tiger and a leopard and two rhinoceros' and we can without trouble throw in a few light monkeys and birds to these heavy articles. It is much cooler here, and we can step out in the evening and walk a few hundred yards undisturbed.'[15] The garden was seen as something ordered, cultivated and a measure of fine taste: 'Barrackpore is a really pretty place. I am making such a garden there, my own private one, for there is a lovely garden there already, but a quarter of a mile from the house, and nobody can walk half a quarter of a mile in this country.'[16] Above all Barrackpore was a haven of privacy where George and she could be alone together, once again, recalling the fun of English days. 'I take a drive or a ride on the elephant alone with George very regularly. I never see him at Calcutta except in a crowd. In short, Barrackpore is, I see, to save me from India.'[17]

One of the boatsmen belonging to the
Governor General's State barge
Sketch by Emily Eden
© Trustees of the Victoria Memorial Hall, Calcutta

we have been making out of a mock-ruin in the garden and there in the midst of our new gold pheasants, which we have imported from China at vast expense to ourselves and vast trouble to _____ _____ (sic) was an immense snake, a sort of serpent, hopping and skipping about the trees in the aviary; 'Quite harmless', the native gardener said, only it was fond of eating birds – our birds – our new birds. He caught it and crammed it into a kedgeree pot, where it was precisely a reel in a bottle. It is all very well, and India is a very nice country but from early and perhaps bad habits I prefer a place where we can go and feed the poultry without finding a great flying serpent whisking and wriggling about.'[19]

While Government House, Calcutta was too public for such domestic activity, in Barrackpore one could take in a few pleasures in the anonymity of a retreat, arranging the flowerbeds, putting up an artistic installation or playing with Chance the dog. Every time Emily arrived at Barrackpore she was struck by the pleasures it afforded. 'Barrackpore is a charming place, like a beautiful English villa on the banks of the Thames - so green and fresh; the house is about the size of Cashiobury, to all appearance, but it just holds George, Fanny and me, the rest of the party all sleep in thatched cottages built in the park; the drawing and dining rooms are immense, and each person requires two or three rooms besides a bath in this country, so as to be able to change rooms from the sun... I see that this place might console me for half the week of Calcutta.'[20] The journey to Barrackpore was done in a luxurious manner aboard the *Soonamookie*, and though Emily, fanned by the cool river breeze fell asleep the instant she was on board, the house was made ready by the four hundred servants including barge-men, kitchen servants and others

By January 1837 the menagerie was well stocked: 'An old tiger, and a young one who is just beginning to turn his playful pats into good hard scratches and is now shut up in a cage grown up and come out, a leopard, two cheetahs, two porcupines, two small black bears, sloths, monkeys...parrots and heaps of beautiful Chinese pheasants.'[18] The exiled Amir Dost Muhammad, taken captive and sent to Calcutta, spent time at Barrackpore and even added animals to the menagerie. In March 1837 Emily was describing the aviary and her newly acquired pheasants from China, considerably enlivening her letters by her descriptions of a sly serpent creeping about and devouring her birds: 'George and I walked to a new aviary or rather pheasantry that

Barrackpore
Charles Hardinge
© Trustees of the Victoria Memorial Hall, Calcutta

Distant view of Barrackpore from Titaghar
Sir Charles D'Oyly
© Trustees of the Victoria Memorial Hall, Calcutta

who were on the towing steamer or the barges 'such a simple way of going to pass two nights in the country.'[21] Elsewhere she grudgingly admitted how this weekly or fortnightly migration was well managed, the Calcutta house is locked up, the establishment travelled to Barrackpore 'and yet ten minutes after we arrive at Government House, everything is in its place.'[22] She made plans for improving the furniture and the servants' liveries' and smartening things up a bit. The boats, elephants, carriages, palanquins took up all attention of the visitors. So Emily, debilitated by the heat, was spared the task of playing hostess.

Sometimes, though, when the weather was agreeable as in December, she relished her Ladyship role. Barrackpore Park donned a festive look as parties were organized for the residents of the Cantonment. 'All the front of the house and the road to the bridge itself were illuminated in a very pretty fashion by Hudson and our own gardener, and the inside of the house was done on my own plan, with arches

of flowers and lamps up the two staircases...the aides-de-camp all turned into tents that were erected in the park, and left their bungalows to the visitors. General Allard and all his Frenchmen came. The Danish people crossed over from Serampore and Calcutta behaved handsomely in furnishing us with sixteen dancing ladies, besides plenty of gentlemen.'[23]

At other times when life was more quiet one could go on elephant rides around the Park or laugh at the resident menagerie - rhinoceros breaking free from its pond and wandering around the grounds, startling the guests. The ponds were dragged for fish and there was much amusement to see the servants scrambling about trying to collect the catch. All night Emily Eden could see little fires spring up around the Park as the servants cooked them. One had to mind the snakes, the sudden storms, the jackals that haunted the garden and carried off the dogs 'Dr. Drummond's little dog has been carried off twice and recovered.' [24] But

Government House and Cenotaph Barrackpore
Sir Charles D'Oyly
© Trustees of the Victoria Memorial Hall, Calcutta

Burial Ground at Barrackpore Emily chanced upon the monument of Jeffrey Amherst and meditated on the large number of tombs of men not older than twenty-five, with monuments erected by friends or brother officers 'and never by relations. By strangers hands his dying eyes were closed, I could not help thinking.'[27] Perhaps an involuntary sigh escaped her as she wryly remarked that they were much too old to die in India.

This was another prophetic thought, for the Eden sisters and George did survive India and returned home in August 1842, though not streaming trails of glory but in disgrace. The handling of the Afghan War had plunged Britain into another unjust and unnecessary war and the rout of the British Army in Afghanistan cast a shadow over their return. Lord Auckland came home to widespread disapproval of his tenure as Governor General.

Lonelier still after the sudden death of Lord Auckland in 1849, and three months later, of Fanny Eden, Emily spent the remainder of her life melancholy and unwell, writing two successful novels but with the zest for living quite gone.

when the rains came 'the river comes nearly up to the house at this time of year, and makes that poor little snivelling Thames look like a miserable dirty drop of a thing.'[25] Emily and George could go out riding in the afternoon by themselves and listen to the band play in the Park every Friday.

In 1836 Emily Eden wrote of looking for a corner in the Park for a school to be built by Lord Auckland at his own expense for Indian children. The school was built in the south-east corner of the Park and was opened in 1837. Emily wrote approvingly on Easter Sunday: 'George's new school has been open this last fortnight, and some of the little native boys already read a fable in one syllable. It is astonishing how quick they are when they choose to learn. I have an idea of giving the monitors, when they have any, a muslin dress apiece.'[26] The school remains till today, a piece of neo-Gothic architecture in a thickly built Bengali town and is known as the Barrackpore Park Government School. Yet the longing for home crept up every now and then, for nothing could quite make up for her long separation from friends and family in England. At the Military

Government House Barrackpore
Sir Charles D'Oyly.
© Trustees of the Victoria Memorial Hall. Calcutta

School at Barrackpore Park, 1851
Frederick Fiebig
© British Library Board

View of Titaghar, Barrackpore in the Distance
Sir Charles D'Oyly.
© Trustees of the Victoria Memorial Hall, Calcutta

Though she had declared in one of her letters that 'I cannot abide India, and that is the truth, and it is almost come to not abiding in India,'[28] perhaps she could not quite escape India. Returning home to England after the exotic life style of the last few years, she had been changed by her encounter with the East. 'Everything is so utterly strange, so much more strange, even than I had expected,'[29] she had said in 1836 when she first arrived in Calcutta and Barrackpore. 'I believe this whole country and our being here, and everything about it, is a dream.'[30]

For Fanny Eden the dream-like scene was viewed as an exotic escapade, as she wrote to a friend in 1836: 'I write and write, because I am determined to believe that you are you, that London is London, that England is England, and that the whole Western world is not a clever and finished fancy of my imagination.'[31] Her India was a series of picturesque events and Indians were viewed as being child like and culturally remote, whose only role was to add to the experience of the sunny East. Life was strung together by ball-room entertainments,

hunts and other sumptuous experiences that had a theatrical, almost showy feel about them.

Emily, on the other hand, felt India and Indians to be vaguely threatening in their strangeness. Many of the letters written from Barrackpore, or describing the camp journey upstream, harp on the difference between what she saw and what her upbringing as an Englishwoman had taught. Undercurrents of race, Empire, violence and death disturbed her continually such as the outline of a temple, the sound of the tom-toms, the screaming to the idols, the idols themselves, 'horrid clay misshapen looking gaudy things,'[32] the dark bloated masses of corpses on the river, the splash of an alligator. The clouds of fire-flies hovering around the boats were comfortless, the coconut trees with their lamps of coconut oil drawn up on the tops of bamboos for religious customs looked 'supernatural'[33] and India was disturbing in its snakes, centipedes, ants, tigers, corpses and black heathen figures. The heat was an externalization of this inner discomfort.

Views from vicinity of Barrackpore
© Victoria Memorial Hall, Calcutta

comfort. The bulbuls and mynahs, the elephants and snakes, the dark skins and veils and heavy jewellery, the quick strange tongues and the brilliant colours were all too alien to be assimilated. For Fanny the strangeness was romance but for Emily it was all too unsettling.

Marian Fowler attempts to redeem Emily Eden by describing how India had bruised her too deeply. When she returned she had hoped to pick up where she had left, but it was too late. She spent more and more time on her sofa, suffering a number of indeterminate ills. She had aged, and so had her beloved George, whilst after his sudden death and Fanny's soon after, Emily Eden's only solace was the memory of her days of laughter in Barrackpore. It was there that with George and Fanny by her side she had come as near to casting off her terrible isolation and exile and live as best as she could.

As Lord Auckland's sister Emily had a steady round of socialising and gaiety to relieve the tedium but as an Englishwoman brought up on the brown earth and pristine woodlands of home, India was too overwhelming in its unfamiliarity to be of much

Pagoda at Eden Gardens
Samuel Bourne
© J Paul Getty Museum, Los Angeles

Paradoxically, India remembers her till today, immortalized in one of the oldest parks in the city of Calcutta, designed in 1841. Both the park and the Eden Gardens stadium at Calcutta are revered landmarks even today.

NOTES

1.   Eden, Emily. 1866. Up The Country: Letters Written to Her Sister From The Upper Provinces of India. R. Bentley.
2.   Fowler, Marian. 1987. Below the Peacock Fan: First Ladies of the Raj. Penguin Books Canada.
3.   Eden, Emily. 1919. 'Letter from King William IV to Miss Eden dated 26th September, 1835.' Miss Eden's Letters. Macmillan and Co. Edited by Violet Dickinson.
4.   Eden, Emily. 1919. 'Letter to Lady Campbell , undated, 1837.' Miss Eden's Letters. Macmillan and Co. Edited by Violet Dickinson.
5.   Eden, Emily. 1919. 'Letter to Mrs Lister dated December 29th, 1836.' Miss Eden's Letters. Macmillan and Co. Edited by Violet Dickinson.
6.   Thackeray-Ritchie, Anne and Evans, Richardson. 1909. Lord Amherst and the British Advance Eastwards Through Burma. University of Oxford.
7.   Eden, Emily. 1866. Up The Country: Letters Written to Her Sister From The Upper Provinces of India. R.Bentley.
8.   Ibid.
9.   Eden, Emily and Eden, Fanny. 1872. Letters from India. Richard Bentley and Son. Edited by Eleanor Eden.
10. Eden, Emily. 1866. Up The Country: Letters Written to Her Sister From The Upper Provinces of India. R.Bentley.
11. Eden, Emily and Eden, Fanny. 1872. Letters from India. Richard Bentley and Son. Edited by Eleanor Eden.
12. Ibid.
13. Eden, Emily. 1919. 'Letter to Mrs Lister dated January 25th, 1837.' Miss Eden's Letters. Macmillan and Co. Edited by Violet Dickinson.
14. Ibid.
15. Ibid.
16. Ibid.
17. Eden, Emily. 1919. 'Letter to Mrs Lister dated March 24th, 1836.' Miss Eden's Letters. Macmillan and Co. Edited by Violet Dickinson.
18. Eden, Emily and Eden, Fanny. 1872. Letters from India. Richard Bentley and Son. Edited by Eleanor Eden.
19. Ibid.
20. Ibid.
21. Ibid.
22. Ibid.
23. Ibid.
24. Ibid.
25. Ibid.
26. Ibid.
27. Ibid.
28. Ibid.
29. Ibid.
30. Ibid.
31. Ibid.
32. Ibid
33. Ibid.

CHAPTER SIX

DARK CLOUDS

❝

"Barrackpore is delightful after Calcutta. We go down there with much the same sensations as those with which you fly from the 'vain city' by railway to the weald of Kent. . . ."

My Indian Peregrinations
The Private letters of Charles Stewart Hardinge

❞

Following the tenures of Lord Ellenborough and Lord Hardinge, Lord Dalhousie arrived in India in 1848. He was accompanied by his wife Susan Hay, a pretty lady whose delicately chiselled features mirror something of her fragile health. From the start Lord Dalhousie had apprehensions of Susan's well-being in India. From his published letters it is clear that he adored her and went to the trouble of setting up a consultation with doctors regarding the arduous journey she would have to undertake. The doctors pronounced that 'a hot climate would not do her harm, and would probably do her good.'[1] Dalhousie set out in November 1847.

The long journey through Egypt was tiring but adventurous. The old Pasha received Lady Dalhousie in an open Durbar and lavished attention upon her which pleased and diverted Lord Dalhousie: '...and there she sat with her cup of coffee and a huge pipe about seven feet long, blowing a distinguished cloud, but blowing it the wrong way, and down the pipe instead of up it.'[2]

Dalhousie is reviled in history as a fierce, if unscrupulous expansionist with his arbitrary appropriation of Indian kingdoms by way of the controversial Doctrine of Lapse. To read these letters is to see another man, one with a puckish humour that is often irresistible. Lord Hardinge, we are told, was shipping home a tiger as a gift for the Queen and Dalhousie observes humorously that the animal might be dangerous, having

Barrackpore House

consumed a large number of men, women and children, as well as being infested with fleas: 'I breathe a fervent and loyal prayer not only for H.M's safety, but that her Majesty may not catch so many fleas from him as my wife did.'[3]

Sometime after their arrival they made the mandatory journey to Barrackpore and were struck by its charms. On 28th February 1848, from aboard the *Soonamookie*, Lord Dalhousie enjoyed the lavish style of travelling, 'in a yacht, all green and gilding, with no crew, towed by a steamer, with sofas and punkahs, and bedrooms and luxuries of all sorts...'[4]

The house itself was pleasing and the parkland was 'charming, and reconciles me to a residence in Bengal more than anything else has yet done. The rooms are large but livable, the furniture not smart but not so scandalous and blackguard as that at the Government House; a pretty pleasure-ground, beautiful garden, an aviary, a menagerie, and all situated on the bank of the river, and surrounded by a park quite home-like in character, and as English as anything can be, where you have banians, and cocoanuts, and palms, and mangoes, for oaks and elms, larch and beech. We propose to spend some days of each week here, and I look for relief and refreshment in it.'[5]

After this initial praise, Dalhousie is reticent about the pleasures of a weekend and his private letters speak of a man possessed by work, almost consumed by it, as he set about making lasting changes in the fabric of Indian life. Dalhousie's rule saw the annexation of Punjab, a war in Burma and the controversial Doctrine of Lapse by which large swathes of Indian territory were summarily added to the British legions. The railways and the telegraph and the imperial post were introduced for quick movement of troops. The superior forms of communication were hoped to help in the creation of British sovereignty. Dalhousie's entire policy in India was driven by the needs of territorial accession and consolidating British might.

James Broun-Ramsay, 1st Marquess of Dalhousie

So was his private life. As in the later half of the 19th century, he used his weekend retreat for his new style of governance, a mixture of authority, expedience and rather simplistic overtures of trust. On the 3rd of April Lady Dalhousie organized a ball for the Barrackpore regiments and in a conciliatory gesture invited native officers. Lord Dalhousie records how 'Some of the old school and some of the young gentlemen did not like this, I believe. I mean to make it the rule; native civilians are invited always, why not native officers?'[6] Sometime later he justifies his invitations by writing, in a surprising moment of perception, that the growing distance between European officers and the native soldiers would lead to much misery, and that it would be a gesture of goodwill on the part of the British to acknowledge the services of the native officers - 'an old Subadar Major - A Sirdar Bahadur, i.e. the highest grade of the Order of India.'[7]

As time passed Dalhousie became increasingly involved in acrimonious disputes with the Court of Directors, with rebellious native states and a turbulent political scenario. Not surprisingly, his tenure began to be hampered by continuous ill health, both his own and Susan's. Repeated references to bad health are found in his letters. In 1849, in a letter from Mussoorie, the Governor General confided how 'I cannot now ride a dozen miles without being worn out; I could not walk two, if I were to be hanged for it.'[8] A visit to Simla did not help matters, for 'Lady D had a second attack of bilious fever'[9] caused by the damp and chill of the station. On 30th May, 1852 in a letter from Barrackpore he writes, 'The considerations of family are more urgent, for my wife's health is already broken again...I am worn and wearied, and though well enough now, I have always before me how emphatically true it is in this country that one knows not what a day may bring forth.'[10]

Duleep Singh
© Alamy Stock Photo

servant of the Company at the Presidency would endure.'[11] Though mindful of the deficiencies in both the houses, he let things be out of deference to Company wishes. In this atmosphere of thrift, the house at Barrackpore continued with its poor and ragged interiors : 'I find the house superb, the furniture disgraceful; an A.D.C's bed absolutely broke down to the ground with him the other day from sheer age; the plate and table equipage very poor...at present John Company has no more cash than his neighbours, and I can't ask much at present.'[12]

Despite the heat and the hindrance Lady Dalhousie kept up the usual appearance of parties and balls. She also, a little unaccountably perhaps, kept a pet bear at Barrackpore who would romp about the rooms and be fed with crumbs; upon her death Lady Canning had to continue the feeding!

Lady Dalhousie's health had never been too strong to start with. In 1842 she had been a Lady of the Bedchamber to Queen Victoria but had resigned due to illness. After trying out various stopovers at Simla and Ceylon, she boarded a steamer for England in 1853, 'Lady D will sail for England in January...we go to Barrackpore next week.'[13]

To his Lordship's great sorrow, she died on the way and with her death Barrackpore ceased to be. Lord Dalhousie immersed himself in his work in an effort to drown out her memory and did not permit himself the luxury of weekend escapes. Perhaps the memories of family time at Barrackpore haunted him. On the 14th of June he broke his brooding silence in an anguished letter 'But I feel all the severity of the scourge, and feel, too, that the circumstances which attend the chastisement have added scorpions to the lash. The severance of two

Like his predecessors, too, Dalhousie was continuously urged by the Court of Directors to be frugal. In another letter he angrily writes how he has saved the Company's money as never before and chosen to ignore the poor trappings of a Governor's life 'though the Government Houses at Calcutta and Barrackpore are furnished as no

Government House Barrackpore,1851
Frederick Fiebig
© British Library Board

souls bound together...is the bitterest drop in the cup of mortality.'[14]

Drowning himself in work, little mention is made of Barrackpore again. Occasional references are made to the guests put up there, including Duleep Singh, Ranjit Singh's youngest son who converted to Christianity quietly with Dalhousie's approval. Sent to Government House before his journey to England, Dalhousie describes him as 'at an awkward age, and has a dark callow down all over his face, but his manners are apparently nice and gentlemanlike, and he now speaks English exceedingly well.'[15] But the rest of the time was spent in profitable expansion, what Dalhousie describes as 'my insatiable rapacity and inordinate expansion.'[16]

Lord Dalhousie did not return to Barrackpore till his daughter Susan Ramsay joined him in January 1855. One assumes that father and daughter found brief moments of happiness there, though Dalhousie himself was seriously ill and almost unfit to move.

On 6th March 1856 Lord Dalhousie left India after receiving the Cannings, broken in health and mind. On that day, in a last letter written from the *Soonamookie*, he says 'Opus exegi - my work is done. I have laid down my scepter, and taking leave of those over whom I ruled, have departed. This evening I embarked and tomorrow shall get to sea...but I am so exhausted with fatigue, agitation and pain, that I can write a very little only.'[17]

When he went to receive his successor at Chandpal Ghat he was almost a cripple, hobbling on crutches. Lady Canning, seeing him in Government House, Calcutta for the first time that day, remarks in her journal how 'Lord Dalhousie came into the drawing room, where I went and sat with him, and - oh how sad to see the change in him, and he is but forty-three! Nothing could be more cheerful and agreeable than I found him, and yet, poor man, how he seemed to be suffering.'[18]

Three years after his departure and while staying in Malta, attempting to revive his health, Lord Dalhousie brushed aside rumours that it was his wanton act of seizing the Kohinoor diamond and sending it as a present to the Queen that had brought him ill luck. 'The Kohinoor has been of ill fortune to the few who lost it. To the long line of emperors, conquerors, and potentates who through successive centuries have possessed it, it has been the symbol of victory and empire...if H.M thinks it brings bad luck, let her give it back to me. I will take it and its ill-luck on speculation.'[19] Yet perhaps it *had* brought him ill fortune. His aggressive policies had certainly brought in waves of resentment which had erupted into the Revolt, thereby putting the fate of the British in India in jeopardy. In 1858 Dalhousie cried out in a letter, 'I am eternally sick, and can neither rest nor sleep...and here, in the midst of the most heavenly weather and scenery, and in the most luxurious quiet, my life is a burden to me every hour of the day and night.'[20]

View of Barrackpore
© RIBA Collections

Aviary in Barrackpore Park , 1851
Frederick Fiebig
© British Library Board

Two years later he died aged only 48. Of his two daughters that survived him, Susan and Edith, Susan's life was as marred by personal tragedy as her father's had been. She returned to India after marrying Robert Bourke, Baron Connemara who served as Governor of Madras between 1886 and 1890 and yet had an acrimonious stay. The Connemara case was one of the great scandals of Victorian society, in which Lord Connemara, a notorious philanderer, is rumoured to have passed on to his wife a sexually transmitted disease. Susan Ramsay took a divorce in 1890 but died eight years later, bitter and childless. Paradoxical too is the fact that though remembered for a range of political and administrative measures that changed India forever, Lord Dalhousie has left no mark on Barrackpore Park. But what Dalhousie failed to do, his successors Lord and Lady Canning more than made up for. Barrackpore Park shone its brightest under the guidance of Lady Canning.

Rhinoceros at Barrackpore Park, 1851
Frederick Fiebig
© British Library Board

Garden at Barrackpore Park, 1851
Frederick Fiebig
© British Library Board

NOTES

1.   Dalhousie, Marquess of. 1910. Private Letters of the Marquess of Dalhousie. William Blackwood and Sons Edinburgh and London. Edited by J.G.A. Baird.
2.   Ibid.
3.   Ibid.
4.   Ibid.
5.   Ibid
6.   Ibid.
7.   Ibid.
8.   Ibid.
9.   Ibid.
10. Ibid.
11. Ibid.
12. Ibid.
13. Ibid.
14. Ibid.
15. Ibid.
16. Ibid.
17. Ibid.
18. Allen, Charles. 1986. A Glimpse of the Burning Plain: Leaves From the Indian Journals of Charlotte Canning. Michael Joseph.
19. op cit Baird
20. Ibid.

CHAPTER SEVEN

THE EYE OF THE STORM

“

“The house faces a great reach of the river, & is crooked
to the bank. I want to set it straight to the eye by making
another walk at the same angle. . . .I have opened to
view a beautiful bunyan, of late hidden by shrubs”

A Glimpse of the Burning Plain
Leaves from the Indian Journals of Charlotte Canning
Charles Allen

”

For long Barrackpore has been synonymous with the figure of Lady Canning. She towers over its history because she loved the house and its gardens the most; indeed, she is its centerpiece and all narratives of Government House lead up to her and away from her. Lord Curzon's 1928 narrative entitled *British Government in India* leads the way in creating this hagiographical portrait. Charles Allen's informative book *A Glimpse of the Burning Plain* which contains excerpts from her letters, drawings and journals completes the romanticizing. The only new note struck is Marian Fowler's recent re-appraisal, a compulsive read which details, amongst other things, Lady Canning's fondness for clothes, jewellery and pomp, her odd moments of racial bias, her quiet evangelizing and her unhappy marriage with the adulterous Lord Canning.

Contemporary gossip had it that the appointment of Canning as Governor General was engineered by old Lord Lansdowne apparently in order to wean him away from his mistress.[1] Lady Canning had been Queen Victoria's Lady of the Bedchamber and it is possible that the Queen approved of Lord Canning's appointment as an escape for her young protégé.

What is clear from contemporary and subsequent narratives is Charlotte Canning's deep attachment to Barrackpore. What is even more poignant is that

View of Osborne, Isle of Wight
William Leighton Leitch, Charlotte Canning
© Royal Collection Trust

this affection, almost unrivalled, was at a time when the Cannings were caught in the nerve-wracking turmoil of the Great Uprising of 1857. This was an event that saw the end of Company rule and power passing officially to the Crown. It was also an irrevocable change in Indian and British relations. Early British historians and chroniclers called the uprising a military rebellion caused by religious fanatics in the British Army. Both Brahmin and Muslim soldiers were incensed by the greased cartridges of the newly introduced Enfield Rifles. Revisionist interpretations, however, pointed out that the quick spread of the rebellion and its virulence of character show that it was possibly an outburst of suppressed anger at British rule. It is beyond the scope of the present work to deal with a political or social analysis of the Rebellion. But significantly the uprising began at Barrackpore, half

a kilometer away from Government House in the Cantonment, and Charlotte Canning's private papers record the ominous signs. Her letters to the Queen provide the British standpoint as well as a spirited defense of her husband's policy of clemency after the revolt was suppressed. Through all the bloodshed and killings stand the gardens at Barrackpore functioning as a psychological refuge, succour and metaphor for Englishness.

Lord and Lady Canning arrived at Calcutta in February 1856, were received by an ailing Lord Dalhousie, went through the usual official engagements, and began to settle in. 'All has become prosperous and quiet. So many great works are in hand that I trust we have much to look forward to cheerfully.'[2] As usual the heat was troubling. Though it was March they had to shut up 'every chink of

Lord Canning at Barnes Court
© Gilman Collection Purchase
Cynthia Hazen Polsky Gift, 2005

Lady Canning
© British Library Board

window from 71/2 A.M, and the venetians outside, and by keeping heavy mats hung up against the outer doors into the court and garden ('compound' here called) just as you see them in Italian churches, we manage to keep the air inside the house pretty cool all day long...'[3]

Lady Canning's first visit to Barrackpore must have been made soon after but was clearly a disappointment. The trees were too green and the park was damp, the house was a 'delabre villa'[4] and the shabby cotton table cloth, Bohemian glass and candlesticks were mean and middle-class. There were snakes on the ground floor where the servants slept and the elephant ride was a novelty but 'not quite a pleasure.'[5]

Lord Dalhousie had stopped visiting Barrackpore after the death of his wife and the house had gone to seed. But the disappointment held out a challenge and Charlotte began the plan of redecorating the House and redoing the garden along the lines of the Governor's House in Parel, Bombay where the Cannings had first landed. 'All my efforts are to try and reach the model of Elphy's establishment but I hardly hope to succeed.'[6]

By October 1856 Charlotte Canning had begun to warm up to Barrackpore. In a letter to the Queen she described how she had begun to 'amuse myself with attempts to make this house comfortable & enliven the drawing room by decorating it with framed sketches, & Your Majesty's last gifts of portraits are surrounded by recollections of Osborne & Balmoral & all my favourite spots at home.'[7] Later on she would decorate the interiors with chintz arm chairs, small round tables and flower pots. 'I really think I have now succeeded in equaling Parel and could invite Elphy himself.'[8]

The careful exhibition of English paintings, chintz and potted plants were imperial markers that

Lord Canning
© Gilman Collection Purchase
Cynthia Hazen Polsky Gift, 2005

Major Bowie, Military Secretary
to Lord Canning, 1860
© Gilman Collection Purchase
Cynthia Hazen Polsky Gift, 2005

inscribed Britain's national identity abroad. Just as Charlotte created a miniature of England in her room decoration she set about to recreate the Barrackpore garden according to memories of her family home at Highcliffe Castle. 'I have now a great deal to improve out of doors, for the garden is badly laid out, though there is a charming terrace walk by the river-side made by Lord Ellenborough...The house faces a great reach of the river, & is crooked to the bank. I want to set it straight to the eye by making another walk at the same angle, & a bank down to the waterside, & I should get a seat on the water's edge of the airiest description. I have opened to view a beautiful bunyan, of late hidden by shrubs.'[9]

But ominous clouds had begun to gather on the horizon, and a fearful storm would soon break. In May 1857 Charlotte Canning wrote in her journal how 'a 34th man at Barrackpore made himself drunk with bang, took a sword and musket & regularly ran amuck. He wounded a sergeant, then stabbed the adjutant's horse & killed him, & wounded the adjutant.'[10] He was taken captive, had since recovered and 'will live to be hanged.'[11]

Mangal Pandey's hanging from a banyan tree in the cantonment area was the spark that ignited the general feeling of disaffection among the Indians. By 11th May, when Charlotte was at Barrackpore for a change of air, Meerut was on fire and the revolting troops were on their way to Delhi. On receiving bad news, Charlotte returned to Calcutta immediately. Barrackpore was protected by the 84th Foot, brought over from Rangoon by Lord Canning, to preside over the disbanding of the regiments there. Patna, Allahabad, Benares, Cawnpore and Meerut had, however, no British troops. Within nine days the Governor General had lost control

The Viscountess Canning, 1858
John Constantine Stanley
© Metropolitan Museum, New York

Mrs Stuart, J.C.S and Mrs d'Aguilar, Barrackpore, 1858
© Lord and Lady Canning Family Album

over a large part of his territory while he remained indecisive over a proclamation assuring the natives that the British meant no harm.

An important source for perceiving the plight of the Cannings' at this point is the collection of letters written by the young ADC Johnny Stanley to his family in England. Johnny had a touching reverence for Lady Canning. His letters home are filled with worshipful accounts of Lady Canning interspersed however with very perceptive remarks. Johnny Stanley, with characteristic wit, describes how Lord Canning was quite out of depth with the Revolt.

'Tell Papa privately that LDC's [Lord Canning] arrears of work are something tremendous, his room is full of boxes not open even, it must be known someday. The officials all over India are at a standstill, they can get no decision, his shaking mouth tells the tale.'[12]

As event after event rolled on, Lord Canning and the British were taken aback by the ferocity of the backlash against the British rulers. Contemporary accounts describe how a disturbed Lord Canning paced round and round the walk at Government House, Calcutta, an endless prowling mirroring the precarious position he now held. The Revolt was less about greased cartridges than it was about Indian disaffection with the outrageous expansionist policies of his predecessors. Caught up in this storm, Lord Canning attempted to instil discipline amongst the British soldiers but was instead blamed for being indecisive and irresolute.

The outward show of normalcy had to be carried on, and the Queen's birthday was celebrated with a gun salute from Fort William in which British redcoats as well as Indian troops were included in a show of trust and loyalty: 'The dotted lines of flashes went duly from end to end, long before I could hear the sound, but I knew then all had gone rightly'[13] wrote Charlotte Canning in her letters. Meanwhile British men-of-war and troops responded to the Governor General's call for help and steamed up the Hooghly bringing veterans like Sir Colin Campbell and Lord Elgin with fleets of warships and men. Rumours were sweeping Calcutta and there were exaggerated accounts of Indian attack, so that 'Revolvers are bought by everyone, & the Freemasons & clerks, & employees of all kinds, want to be formed into regiments and yeomanry. There is not the least cause of fear here, & it is absurd to see how people who ought to know better set an example of fear, which must have a bad effect on natives.'[14] Charlotte learnt of the bloodshed and violence from other British administrators, like the surgeon Dr Leckie or Major Bowie. It is also possible that her breathless letters to Queen Victoria keeping her informed of the

Lady Canning and J.C.S, Barrackpore
Unknown 1858-61
© Gilman Collection, Purchase
Cynthia Hazen Polsky Gift, 2005

Lady Canning on her Black Arab and Lord Clyde
Commander-in-Chief
Gilman Collection, Purchase,
Cynthia Hazen Polsky Gift, 2005

crisis had the tacit approval of Lord Canning who relied heavily on his wife's closeness to the Queen to provide a comforting account of himself.

Lady Canning busied herself with relief work as European refugees from up the country poured into Calcutta, 'making a collection of clothes to send to the houses of the destitute arrivals'[15] or visiting the wounded troops. Photographs of Lady Canning taken at this time show her comforting the survivors of the siege of Lucknow and Cawnpore. Interestingly Lady Canning and Florence Nightingale had been old friends, and though Florence Nightingale had offered assistance, Charlotte wrote to the Queen that 'I am sure her offer is hearty & true, but it would be wrong to encourage her to come.'[16] Quite inexplicably, Charlotte had expected the fighting to be over soon.

By September, the worst of the Revolt for the British was over. The siege of Lucknow and Cawnpore was still a nightmarish memory but English troops had begun to arrive in large numbers to beat off the sepoys. While British hearts grew easy, the terrible English reprisal had begun, but for Charlotte Canning that mattered little.

She returned to Barrackpore and found it the same Arcadia she had left months ago, with gardeners laying out new beds '...a great many groups of plants with brilliant flowers near the pools & tanks, & above all the new terrace-most successful.'[17] She plunged herself into her old pastimes, sketching, designing, visiting the aviary, redecorating the house.

The paintings made by her of Barrackpore in this period, found in the collections at Harewood House and the Victoria & Albert Musuem are startling in their intensity. One can almost picture the spare figure of Charlotte Canning, childless, unhappy in her marriage, intensely lonely, in an alien country gripped by war, setting up her easel in the garden or on the river bank and covering sheet after sheet with paint and brush to alleviate her grinding misery. Her perceptive ADC Johnny Stanley in a series of lively letters home to his mother remarked 'I do not like the way the G.G. treats Lady Canning, she is so constantly thinking of him only & how to please him and he is as sulky as possible.'[18] As a thing of convenience which produced no heir their marriage was difficult, with the Revolt raging in the background and the British almost out of their depth in trying to deal with it, it could only have got worse. Barrackpore was Charlotte Canning's refuge.

Today the house and park are greatly changed. Those who visit the area would take delight in following Charlotte Canning's art trail, looking

Banyan tree near the House, Barrackpore
Charlotte Canning
© By kind permission of the Harewood House Trust

through her eyes, out of the verandah onto the river, the main gate of the Park sketched on her first visit, the wooded paths, her refurbished drawing room and the great banyan tree. Interestingly, though the riverside walk was modelled along the formal symmetry of English parks, the grounds were too English for her. 'The Park is beautifully planted with round headed trees to look as English as possible - more so than I can approve, and I am glad when Bamboos & Cocoanuts & Palms have crept in.'[19]

Her letters and journals of this period had previously held vivid accounts of the sepoy killings at Lucknow and Cawnpore, of the counter-attack by General Havelock and the new Commander-in-Chief Colin Campbell. Now they described the English victory and the Queen's Proclamation. It was in Barrackpore that news of British triumph reached her. She had been overseeing reconstruction at her balustrade verandah when news reached her of the fall of Delhi. She rejoiced with Sir Campbell and prepared to return to Calcutta but not before a private rejoicing,

From the Verandah at Barrackpore
Charlotte Canning
© By kind permission of the Harewood House Trust

calming herself by walking through her beloved garden. 'It was a grey pleasant day, and I ventured a little with an umbrella, under the great Banyan & about some walks – a thing I had never done at that hour before. I was well repaid. The whole place was alive with the most gorgeous butterflies, of all sizes & colours, & shapes. The orchids in the Banyan are in brilliant health, and I am only sorry to think that except for a day at a time, we shall have no enjoyment of that charming spot. As the elephants were at the door long before the carriage, we got upon them for a ride to the park gate. Punch would have made a nice vignette of Sir Colin with me in a howdah on the top of an elephant, talking over our great news in the greatest delight.'[20]

Lord Canning meanwhile had decided to move his administration temporarily to Allahabad in order to oversee the job of reconstruction. Charlotte Canning found herself, characteristically, alone and in December she celebrated New Year's Eve by attending a fete for the children of the British troops. 'I never felt more glad of the end of any year than of the last terrible and unhappy one,'[21], she wrote in her journal.

In January Lord Canning left for Allahabad and in March 1858 Charlotte left for a tour of the Nilgiris. She could meet Lord Canning only in July when she reached Allahabad also, and the rest of 1858 and 1859 was spent in undertaking a long and arduous camp to Lucknow, Cawnpore, Lahore, Simla and Mussoorie.

Charlotte Canning returned to Barrackpore for a few weeks in 1860 and finally in 1861. Contemporary accounts describe how these visits were the only thing in their Viceregal life that Lady Canning cared for. 'We used to sit in the upper verandah, facing the river with a lovely view before

Soonamookie by Charlotte Canning
© Victoria and Albert Museum, London

us, and the verandah itself full of beautiful flowers brought for her to paint; and on cooler days, we sat under the great banyan tree in the private garden, reading and working and talking.'[22]

What could be the source of Lady Canning's great attachment to Barrackpore? For a start it gave her a sense of being, the joy of creating what she perceived as her private garden and house, fuelled by subconscious remembrances of her childhood gardens at Cambridgeshire, at St Albans and at Highcliffe Castle, Hampshire. One might also speculate that her solitude was intense, as it had been for most Governors' wives, but more extreme because of the lack of socializing that the Revolt and its aftermath provoked. Lord Minto could enjoy a *nautch*, the Edens entertained and socialized and had themselves for company, while the later Vicereines had more of an extended family as well as the newly created Western educated Indians to socialize with, albeit with condescension. Charlotte Canning was caught in a cusp where earlier intimacies were discouraged but the later, more sophisticated forms of socializing, like *zenana* parties or charity events were not yet discovered. The rigours of her position meant a deliberate distancing from Indian as well as English society; in any case she disliked going to the *maidan* for the customary

Tomb of Charlotte Canning with a view of the Hooghly River in the distance, 1869
Sir Michael Anthony Shrapnel Biddulph
© Royal Collection Trust

evening drive and 'round and round the course bowing to all the beau monde'[23] was not a pleasure. Johnny Stanley reported guardedly in 1858 that he had been told by several persons that Lady Canning was not all pious duty and affection: 'I have only seen her bright side and that last year she used to be very cold and proud.'[24]

Added to Charlotte Canning's despondence was Lord Canning's evident distancing from her, both at a personal level and because of the sheer burden of administrative worries once the Revolt broke out. Lord Canning, thought Johnny Stanley, was troubled during the Revolt because he was essentially weak; 'His mouth has gone in more as he never wears his false teeth now.'[25]

Increasingly Lord Canning stayed at Government House, Calcutta or up the country while Charlotte Canning remained in Barrackpore, pottering about the garden under a scarlet umbrella with a train of servants taking instructions, sketching, painting, touching up the drawings on her verandah. As she lived her lonely life the boats and barges crossed the Hooghly outside her window, busy in the work of empire.

Tomb of Lady Canning at Barrackpore, 1861
© Gilman Collection, Purchase, Cynthia Hazen Polsky Gift, 2005

In 1858 Charlotte Canning began a series of arduous camps that would make her criss-cross India, from Lahore to Simla, from Delhi to the Tibetan border at Chini, from Allahabad to Coonoor. A keen amateur botanist as well as an artist, the fruits of such tours can be seen in her portfolios of sketches that have survived. In her sketches we wonder at the long miles covered, the enormous distances traversed on palanquins and ponies and elephants and tonjons, her journey on the *Soonamookie*, with its large convoy of barges. 'Intensely interesting' said Queen Victoria in a letter remarking on her adventurous posts, 'but I think much of it sounded very dangerous.'[26]

Lord Canning was due to return to England in 1862 and Lady Canning spent her last few months between Calcutta and Barrackpore with a newly made friend Emily Bayley, wife of the temporary Foreign Secretary Edward Bayley. The long awaited

Tomb of Charlotte Canning, Barrackpore, 1870
Francis Firth
© Victoria and Albert Museum, London

return to England had made her warm and mellow, and as she walked along the river, sat under the banyan tree, sketched on the verandah and tidied up her scrapbooks and portfolios there was a sense of melancholy at leaving Barrackpore behind: 'I shall be quite low at parting with that really nice place, and have greatly enjoyed there the command of a tropical garden, where one orders all sorts of hothouse flowers, in groves, and hedges, and thickets. I have literally a double hedge of poinsettia, which will be in a month or two a scarlet wall, and one of dark ipomoea.'[27]

She was never to return home, of course. In October 1861 Lady Canning set off on an expedition to the newly developing hill station of Darjeeling which she had longed to visit and see the highest mountain in the world. In her letters written to Lord Canning, the only ones to survive, she describes the wonderful luxuriance of the woods and mountains. In November, on her way back to Calcutta she contracted malaria in the *terai*. In Calcutta she suffered for eight days before passing into a coma and dying on 18th November.

Tomb of Charlotte Canning
© Alamy Stock Photo

In a letter to Queen Victoria dated 22nd November Lord Canning wrote 'The Funeral is over. It took place quite privately at sunrise on the 19th. There is no burial place for the Governor General or his Family, and the Cemeteries at Calcutta are odious in many ways. Lord Canning has therefore set a portion of the garden at Barrackpore apart for the purpose. It is a beautiful spot; - looking upon that reach of the grand river which she was so fond of drawing - shaded from the glare of the sun by high trees, and amongst the bright shrubs and flowers in which she had so much pleasure.'[28]

Lady Canning's body was laid to rest in a corner of her beloved Barrackpore, at a point where the view caught the river and the riverside walk that had so delighted her while she lived. Significantly, the burial took place at daybreak and was an intensely private ceremony where no one except Lord Canning and the Viceroy's household staff were present. Lord Canning, the ADCs and the Commander of the Bodyguard acted as pall bearers. The Indian sentries were kept outside the garden and none from European society was informed. Lord Canning clearly intended to keep

Tomb of Charlotte Canning at St. John's Church, Calcutta

his wife's last rites a moment of very personal mourning. Moreover, he had also intended to start a burial place fit for the Governor General and his family away from the 'odious' cemeteries of Calcutta. Barrackpore Park, with its associations of a secluded spot for the governing elite, was the perfect place. The thought remained unfulfilled, but the Park continued to be a private site for the Viceroys.

Lord Curzon's account of the burial is a soulful and highly overwrought account in which Curzon filtered the event through his own intense romanticising of the past. 'Lady Canning had died at Government House Calcutta; and there at midnight on the day of her death the four ADCs of the Viceroy, one of whom long afterwards told me the tale, lifted her body into the coffin, which was carried on a gun-carriage, drawn by six black horses to Barrackpore in the dead of the Indian night. In the breaking dawn of the next morning, while the full moon was setting in one quarter of the heavens, and the first rays of the sun struggled up the Eastern sky and faintly flushed the silent stream, the body was carried down the terraced walk from Government House on the shoulders of twelve English soldiers, the ADCs holding the fringe of the pall. Lord Canning walked immediately after, the stricken figure of a doomed man, eleven persons only were present at the ceremony, which was conducted by the Archdeacon of Calcutta. A solid masonry vault had been constructed by Captain [afterwards Sir Henry] Yule, Secretary of the Public Works Department, by the side of the terraced walk, at a spot where Lady Canning had loved to sit; and there the body of this beautiful and ill-fated woman was laid to rest.'[29] The inscription on the headstone was composed by Lord Canning on the third day after her death. A temporary structure was erected to protect the grave. Lord Canning may have been indifferent in life but was acutely dutiful to his wife after her death, for it was said that he visited his wife's grave as often as he could to place flowers on it.

Later Bishop Cotton consecrated the ground in 1862. By the time the tomb inscription was graven in stone, another life had gone. Lord Canning survived his wife by only seven months, dying of liver abscesses upon his return to England. Twenty years earlier, Emily Eden had lamented on the death of a friend who had died of liver failure, saying that 'he died of abscess on the liver – of India, in fact.'[30] Lord Canning, like Lord Dalhousie and Lord Auckland before him, and Lord Elgin after, died 'of India'. All had untimely deaths perhaps because of the difficult toil in an unfamiliar climate that their job involved.

Lady Canning's tomb monument in Barrackpore was designed by her sister Louisa Waterford and erected three years after her death. Till then the grave lay with a temporary brick covering and flowers were heaped over it in the form of a cross. The monument was a marble platform ornamented with inlaid mosaic which began to degenerate so much in the extreme climatic conditions that in 1873, it was shifted to Calcutta and placed at St Paul's Cathedral. A replica was made and raised over the Barrackpore grave where it is still to be seen. The original found its final resting place at the St John's Church in Calcutta. Meanwhile photographs of the Barrackpore site began to circulate from the 1860s. The first photographs were possibly taken by Lady Emily Bayley, Charlotte's close friend. Later photographs show the marble monument, the trees shading the grave and, in a final evocation of the picturesque, the gardens on either side and the river glimmering in the distance. Like the Cawnpore memorial at the Bibighar, the grave became an iconic reminder of the irreparable loss of lives made in the service of England.[31]

The iron railing at Barrackpore, with its interwoven CCs, was lost over time. A suggestion was made by a visitor from the Lutyens Trust to the present writers that the iron may have been melted and used in World War II for making field guns as was done elsewhere to arm the Allied Forces; though the veracity of the suggestion cannot be made, it would point to the breakdown of the old world order that the 20th century style of combat enjoined.

A port called Canning, envisioned in 1857 to be built on the River Matla at the mouth of the Ganges delta, near the Sunderbans never took off, though the town of the same name continues to survive and is two hours away from Calcutta. But Lady Canning remains special to Bengalis because of a sweet called *ledikeni* named after her and savoured by all till today. Lord Canning's statue, installed outside Government House, Calcutta, was removed in the late sixties of the last century as part of the

Watercolour drawing from an album of topographical views in India by Lady Charlotte Canning, 1858
© Victoria and Albert Museum, London

project of colonial erasure. At a time when other British statues were banished to the lawns of the Flagstaff House, someone, somewhere placed it at Barrackpore, overlooking his wife's tomb, mindful of the pathos of the situation.

Tomb and statue stand today, a gloomy memorial to all the lives that Empire took.

NOTES ————————————————————————————————

1. Allen, Charles. 1986. A Glimpse of the Burning Plain: Leaves From the Indian Journals of Charlotte Canning. Michael Joseph.
2. Ibid.
3. Ibid.
4. Ibid.
5. Ibid.
6. Ibid.
7. Surtees, Virginia. 1975. Charlotte Canning. John Murray
8. Allen, Charles.
9. Ibid.
10. Ibid.
11. Ibid.
12. Mitford, Nancy. 1939. The Stanleys of Alderley: Their Letters Between the Years 1851-1865. Hamish Hamilton Ltd.
13. Allen, Charles.
14. Ibid.
15. Ibid.
16. Ibid.
17. Surtees, Virginia.
18. Mitford, Nancy.
19. Surtees, Virginia.
20. Allen, Charles.
21. Ibid.
22. Ibid.
23. Ibid.
24. Mitford, Nancy.
25. Ibid.
26. Allen, Charles.
27. Allen, Charles.
28. Surtees, Virginia.
29. George Curzon, The Marquis Kedleston K.G. 1925. British Government in India: The Story of the Viceroys and Government Houses. Cassel and Company Ltd.
30. Eden, Emily. 1866. Up The Country: Letters Written to Her Sister From the Upper Provinces of India. R. Bentley.
31. Anderson, Tracy. 2013. 'The Lives and Afterlives of Charlotte, Lady Canning (1817-1861): Gender, Commemoration and Narratives of Loss.' South-Asian Studies. Vol 29. Issue 1. Republished in The Afterlives of Monuments by Cherry, Deborah. Routledge.

CHAPTER EIGHT

THE MOUNTAINS BECKON

"

*"In truth Barrackpore had lost its main raison d'etre.
With the consecration of Simla as the summer capital
of India beginning in the mid-1860s, Barrackpore was
demoted to something closer to Chequers or
Camp David... "*

Flora's Empire
British gardens in India
Eugenia W Herbert

"

In 1858 the East India Company's Indian possessions were given over to the British Crown. The Crown itself was acquiring a mysterious symbolic power through the figure of Britain's iconic monarch Queen Victoria. Though a constitutional head without any real say in administration, the Queen nevertheless had become an emblem of Britishness, in her devotion to Prince Albert, her large family of nine children and later, after Albert's death, her austere withdrawal from public life as she mourned for him and gave rise to the Victorian obsession with death.

Meanwhile the British empire had increased vastly and now included, at the height of its power, far-flung territories including India, the Caribbean, parts of Africa, Australia, New Zealand and Canada. It now controlled most of the major economic resources of the world including rubber, tea, sugar, gold and diamonds, cotton and jute. Economic powers were cloaked by racist and paternalistic attitudes and a new self consciousness of purpose that colonial rule now believed in. Life itself was moving from the grim starkness of the early 19th century to the comforts and conveniences of modern

Queen Victoria, Empress of India, 1877
Bourne & Shepherd
© J Paul Getty Museum, Los Angeles

sea. The Red Sea route, although opened by the East India Company by the 1820s, had been still depressingly long, as reflected in Emma Roberts' memoirs, and included a precarious ride through the desert on donkey chairs. By the 1850s matters had improved and one could travel along the Canal in a small steamer to Suez and then on to Bombay. By the 1870s transatlantic steamers made travelling easy and the P&O steamships were glamorous modes carrying a veritable who's who of civil servants, army men and wives.

Another great leap to the modern era was made by photography, which became the new rage from the mid 19th century onwards. The water colours and sketches of Lady Loudon, Lady Amherst, Fanny Eden and her sister Emily Eden were replaced by sepia prints. Lady Canning began the trend of taking photographs and by 1867 Samuel Bourne had taken the first photographs of Barrackpore Park.

inventions including railways, transatlantic steamships and the transatlantic telegraph cable that began working from 1866.

In India the hazards of the climate continued and life was still difficult for the British, but the new transport systems meant ease in communication and travel. In Lord Amherst's time dispatches and letters had taken half a year to travel from London to Calcutta. By 1852 cable connections could transmit messages within two days while letters from London to Calcutta would reach in about forty-four days. The journey to India was also no longer a toilsome affair of four or six months by

Samuel Bourne
© Royal Collection Trust

Lord Mayo Lying in State
Alexander Caddy
© Trustees of the Victoria Memorial Hall, Calcutta

India had also changed after the disturbances of 1857. The native states had finally been beaten down and there were no 'lions' in Mysore or the Punjab anymore. The brutalities at Cawnpore and Lucknow were exorcised repeatedly through Revolt literature and reminiscences as well as monuments, like the one set up at the Cawnpore Well. British life in India was now in a state of sanctimonious self-importance, described as the High Raj of self-conscious solemnity. There was a sense of superiority, bolstered by a mass of rituals such as *durbars*. There was a completely self-contained English society who made annual migrations to the hills to escape the heat. Finally there was a sense of carrying out the business of Empire as a duty to the people of India.

But the one aspect of India that was still unsettling was its suddenness. Every European in India walked in the valley of death. Its shadow was everywhere

Elgin's tomb in Dhurmsala, 1868
Samuel Bourne
© J Paul Getty Museum, Los Angeles

Views of Barrackpore Park
Samuel Bourne
© Royal Collection Trust

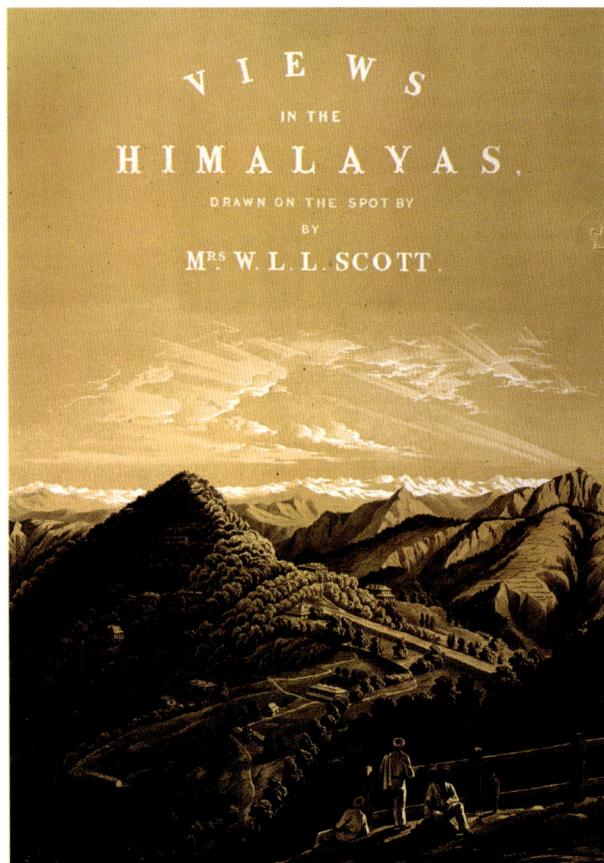

The first view of Simla
© The British Library Board

Lord Canning had barely time to call upon the Queen on arrival in England after burying Lady Canning at Barrackpore before dying himself six weeks after. The first Lord Elgin had died of a heart attack suffered while crossing a rope bridge near Dharamshala and was buried there two days later. Lord Minto had been within a few miles of home in Scotland when he died of pneumonia and Lord Mayo had been killed by an Afghan convict in the Andaman Islands. Climate, elaborate meals unsuited to the heat, too many balls, levees, *durbars* and the long dusty trail of camp-life left them ill and disoriented.

In the early years, in the 17th and 18th centuries, Governors fashioned retreats as best as they could on the outskirts of their towns. Madras had a second Government House at Guindy, Bombay had Malabar Hills in addition to Parel. As the British expanded in India so did their search for retreats in cooler climes and the answer was found in the hills at Simla where a Lieutenant Ross had built the first cottage on its balmy slopes in 1819. In 1827 Lord Amherst travelled to Simla to escape from the heat, thus starting off a fashion followed by his successors.

The settlement of Simla was a fortunate consequence of Hastings' war with Nepal, by which the British acquired many hill-stations including Musoorie, Naini Tal, Ranikhet and Simla. In 1822, Captain Charles Kennedy built a house there which, according to Jan Morris, looked more like a forest temple than a residence.

By 1838, in spite of the difficulties in reaching there, Emily Eden declared it to be a beautiful place with its rhododendrons, violets, pine trees and general feeling of gaiety.

and upon everyone, from Viceroy to soldier and was often unsettling and violent. A man or woman could be 'chatting pleasantly at breakfast, struck down by cholera at noon, dead by evening.'[1] Calcutta's very own Job Charnock, credited with transforming three villages into a settlement that would evolve into a premier city, died after living a full life in 1693, when he was in his sixties, but his only son predeceased him in an untimely death. An aging Lord Cornwallis, returned by the Court of Directors for a second innings in 1805, died within two months of arrival. Lord Dalhousie came to India sprightly and full of verve at the age of thirty five and left it a shell of a man when forty.

Simla; The Yarrows with Shalli Peaks in the Background, 1868
Samuel Bourne
© J Paul Getty Museum, Los Angeles

From 1864, Sir John Lawrence, Viceroy after Canning, routinely travelled to Simla and established it as the summer capital from April to November. His predecessors had spent one or two hot seasons in the hills, leaving the Council and Secretariat behind in Calcutta, but Lawrence insisted on moving the entire Viceroyalty to Simla. One reason for this was his poor health, the other was political expedience in controlling the North after the Revolt. As the only civilian who had worked his way up to a Viceroy, perhaps psychologically Simla was closer to him than Calcutta. He had worked in the Punjab in 1857 during the Revolt and had been instrumental in keeping Punjab on the British side.

In Calcutta Lawrence felt hemmed in by convention, and frequently shocked the strict Calcutta society with his informal ways which included walking to church and wandering around the native parts of the town incognito. 'He would mingle with the crowds in the bazaars, his knowledge of Indian languages enabling him to hear what people were saying about him.'[2]

In Simla, with its robust climate and familiar environs, Lawrence felt at home. What Lawrence had begun could not be undone. As time passed, Simla became a haunt for the British in summer. British residents arrived in droves and the station became filled with civilians on leave, bored wives

John Laird Mair Lawrence, 1st Baron Lawrence
Maull & Polyblank
© National Portrait Gallery, London

Governor of Punjab and the Commander-in-Chief clattering up and down. Apart from these three, no one was permitted to use carriages in Simla.

The years moved on and Barrackpore and its house became more and more distant to the Viceroy, perhaps used as a quick getaway in winter but clearly upstaged by the bungalows and houses at Simla, by Peterhof and later the imposing Viceregal Lodge built on Observatory Hill.

Occasionally we get glimpses of an escape to Government House, Barrackpore. In 1874 Lord Northbrooke cancelled the migration to Simla and spent weekends at Barrackpore to economise at a time when a terrible famine was sweeping through the country. For Lord Lytton, however, Simla was the preferred destination. With its parties and tennis courts, the wondrous balls at Peterhof, and the lavish costumes of the Dramatic Society theatricals afterwards, Simla was a golden glittering world of raffish splendour far from the burning plains. However, when she finally arrived in Calcutta nine months after coming to India, Edith Lytton was enchanted by the house at Barrackpore and whenever possible tried to stay there, with 'meals out under the arches of a great banyan tree'[4] or visiting schools and the wives of the British soldiers stationed there. But these stays were few; indeed the Lyttons seemed to have spent most of their time in Simla. However, they made some improvements to the house. A stone staircase was built on the south verandah and a wooden portico was built at the southern entrance. Sadly the portico has been lost over time.

The Marchioness of Ripon planted a bamboo avenue which was immortalized in photographs, its leafy trellis providing a welcome shade to guests

of officers recuperating as their husbands toiled in the plains below, rich businessmen from Calcutta and others who chose to settle there. It was, as Kipling proclaimed in his poem *The Lovers Litany*, the place for glamour, wine and witchery. *The Complete Indian Housekeeper* warned that 'no one should go up that has not a bag of rupees and many pretty frocks.'[3] Certainly Simla was picturesque enough to emulate England, with its winding roads, cottages hung with lace curtains, its Gothic church, its rickshaws and the carriages of the Viceroy, the

Bamboo Avenue, Barrackpore, 1889
© The Trustees of the Bowood Collection

as they walked from the landing ghat to the house. Barrackpore bloomed briefly, during the time of Lady Dufferin. Subsequently during the time of Henry Petty - Fitzmaurice, the fifth Marquess of Lansdowne from 1888 to 1894 it was put to good use. Later, during the tenure of the Ninth Earl of Elgin in the 1890s Barrackpore was special to his daughter Lady Elizabeth Bruce because it was in Simla, as well as here that her future husband Henry Babington-Smith wooed her in successful dalliance, under the banyan tree and in the garden where they had all gone to celebrate his birthday: 'The mango trees and lilies and violets are so fresh after the rain. H.E. sang some songs after dinner and Mr. B.S gave me reed pens to draw with.'[5]

Yet such vivid moments were infrequent and the truth was that the great days of the house were over. Almost over. In 1899 Lord Curzon rediscovered Government House, Barrackpore and gave it one last triumphal blaze of glory. His successor, Minto, kept up the show, but already the die was cast. In 1912, when the capital was shifted to Delhi under Lord Hardinge, Wellesley's grand mansion, once majestic in conception and loved by many rulers, had dwindled into a shabby old toy, forgotten after play.

NOTES

1. Fowler, Marian. 1987. Below the Peacock Fan: First Ladies of the Raj. Penguin Books Canada
2. Bence-Jones, Mark. 1982. The Viceroys of India. Constable.
3. Steel, Flora-Annie and Gardiner, Grace. 1898. The Complete Indian Housekeeper and Cook. William Heinemann.
4. Lutyens, Mary. 1979. The Lyttons in India. John Murray.
5. de Courcy, Anne. 2013. The Fishing Fleet. Windsor.

CHAPTER NINE

UNAMBIGUOUS AFFECTION

❝

"The afternoon was lovely, and we enjoyed it very much, as we sat under the banian-tree waiting for D and our guests"

Our Viceregal Life in India
The Marchioness of Dufferin & Ava

❞

India could bring out the best and worst in the memsahib. While Emily Eden's letters from India were lively and peppered with caustic observations on life and manners, they could also be waspish and high-handed. Particularly tedious were her constant references to loneliness, discomforts of the weather and the desire to be home.

With Hariot, the Marchioness of Dufferin and Ava, the letters change in tone to a sophisticated cosmopolitanism characteristic of the wife of a career diplomat. While Emily Eden had never been beyond England before she set out for India in her late thirties, Hariot Dufferin was a true diplomat's wife, known for her hospitality and service as she accompanied her husband to Canada, St Petersburg, the Ottoman Empire, India, Paris and Rome. When she arrived in India she was well travelled,

purposeful and had a clearer idea of her role as a Vicereine than her predecessors. This is reflected in the urbane and polished note in her letters. Like her predecessors she recorded her impressions of India for posterity through journals, letters and in her case, photographs as against the sketches and watercolors of Charlotte Canning and Emily Eden. Many tomes have been written on the use of photographs as imperial discourse, arranging subjects and carefully filtering and distancing disturbing feelings. The photographs of Hariot Dufferin show her sense of style and her confident air as she photographed Indian landscapes, scenery and Indians, all however suitably arranged to show her privileged status.

Lady Dufferin's journal contains letters written to her mother Catherine Anne Rowan Hamilton. These

Annapurna Temple near the South Gate of Barrackpore Park
© Manotosh Paul

were printed at the Viceregal Press and circulated amongst her family and friends. These letters became the basis for her two volume travel account entitled *Our Viceregal Life in India*. The letters are a record of her observations on her life as a Vicereine and thus duly report on her daily pursuits of reading, playing tennis, attending picnics and parties and all the other expected pursuits of an Englishwoman in India. But these letters are not so much an actual intimate exploration of daily minutiae as a documentation of actions expected to be held up as worthy and appropriate. In her study on Hariot Dufferin, Eadaoin Agnew has discussed how the establishment of an anglicised home was an obligation

that kept memsahibs busy because they felt that in creating an English domestic space, one could contribute to colonial control in India.[1] The plethora of servants also meant that there was free time for travel and writing which were seen as appropriate actions of a cultivated woman.

The process was complicated by Queen Victoria who portrayed herself as a mother with a large brood of children and a compatible husband, as well as a mother to all her colonies. The mother image was therefore carried forward to include the metaphorical space of Empire. In this, Queen Victoria was seen as a *maharani* as well as a mother

Hariot Dufferin

Lord Dufferin

figure to all Britain's subjects. This 'maternal imperialism' of someone who liked to call herself the 'Empress of India' and who could actively manage private and public life had to be duplicated. Most Vicereines sought to reproduce this graceful blend of matriarch and benevolent ruler in their lives as a memsahib.

Hariot Dufferin played the role to effortless perfection, moving from a Government House hostess to presiding over school visits, prize-giving ceremonies and hospital work. The Lady Dufferin Fund which was set up by her pioneered female healthcare in India. Her journal provides interesting insights into the funding and creation of the Fund, as well as Lady Dufferin's interest in related areas

like female education. On Friday the 27th of February 1885 she was in Chinsurah for a prize giving ceremony. 'The function consisted in listening to much Bengali poetry repeated by little girls'[2] and on Wednesday the 11th of March she wrote, 'I went off to lay the foundation-stone of a home for girls studying medicine. The money for it has been given by the Maharanee Surnomoyee, who seems to be a most charitable lady.'[3] Visiting Bethune School, she was struck by 'the nice face of the first B.A;'[4] this was Kadambini Ganguly who later trained as one of India's first female doctors.

Breathlessly rushing from *zenana* visits to school inspections and prize ceremonies, the Dufferins were also noted for their splendid Viceregal

Lord Dufferin in Barrackpore Park
© Getty Images

entertainments at Calcutta, Simla and Barrackpore. In 1885 the Barrackpore house, though well past its prime, was once again being used for quick weekend parties. On Sunday the 8th of February a large garden party included 'Sir Charles and Lady Macgregor, Sir Auckland Colvin, Lord Randolph Churchill, and two Frenchmen... They all liked their day in the country, and all thought Barrackpore perfectly lovely.'[5]

Barrackpore was an important centre of entertainment for the Dufferins and pages in the journal are devoted to detailing the pleasures of the garden retreat there. 'D, and the rest of the party went off in the launch directly after breakfast for the Viceroy is hard at work all and every day and has to hurry back to his office early on Monday morning but I remained behind for a couple of hours, which I spent in arranging all the rooms for the duke and duchess of Connaught, who come to

stay with us next week.'[6] And next week: 'Lady Downe, the Bishop, Major Cooper, and I going up in the launch to Barrackpore. I was anxious to see that all was in order for our guests, and I was rewarded for giving up the races by having a nice quiet afternoon.'[7]

There is unambiguous affection in Hariot's appreciation of the house and park. The indefatigable military secretary William Beresford had introduced its charms on Christmas Day 1884. As Hariot records: 'Lord William Beresford had suggested that we should go and see Barrackpore in the afternoon, and as we were very glad to find some way of spending our Christmas with an appearance of gaiety we arranged to do so. We started in the steam launch as soon after church as possible and enjoyed the trip up the river very much. With Barrackpore we were quite delighted... it is situated on the river, and is quite like an English

Viceregal Lodge, Simla

park, with beautiful single trees of different kinds, and it is all so pretty and so completely in the country that I long to go and stay there. It reminds me of the Duke of Westminster's place on the Thames, Cliveden, and we happened to have two of his sons with us who thought so too...'[8]

She describes the short walk arched over by bamboos, the garden with a fountain in it, the lawn filled with shrubbery, 'strange plants' and the banyan tree 'covering a great space of ground, its branches and off-shoots forming arches and galleries, and a fine dining room, which we used for luncheon. The scarlet liveries looked very beautiful moving in and out of this natural arbour, and we fell in love with Barrackpore on the spot.'[9]

Elaborate suppers and large parties were part of the imperial display. Hariot Dufferin speaks of state dinners and receptions held for the weekend guests afterwards at the Calcutta house. After the rebellion of 1857 so much had changed, and where previously wives like Charlotte Canning and Lady Amherst thought it tiresome to indulge in so much of gaiety and abandon, now they were tasked with transporting British culture and society to India. Just as the guidance books like Flora Annie Steele and Grace Gardiner's manual of practical advice evoked the energetic strong female partner as the bulwark of the Empire, so also were colonial wives expected to exemplify British superiority through productive activity. And what a hive of activity it was! 'The girls and I came down to Barrackpore

View from the Government House, Barrackpore, 1858
© Gilman Collection, Purchase
Cynthia Hazen Polksy Gift, 2005

Barrackpore in the mid-19th Century
Francis Firth
© Victoria and Albert Museum

early by train, as I wanted to see the institutions here. They are of a nice small size, so that a little tea and tobacco and a plum cake are sufficient to give pleasure. Four very old women are entirely provided for, and there are a few other pensioners and a school for native Christian children. There were some fascinating infants there, and the teaching seemed wonderfully good. The pupils, who had only been learning a year, wrote English and Hindusthani characters remarkably well, and they sang in English, pronouncing it most distinctly.'[10]

This was 1885 and Hariot Dufferin could not fail to notice the rising tide of nationalism, especially since Lord Dufferin was much beset by the problem of whether to ignore the growing disaffection amongst the educated Indians or show understanding of their demands. Hariot was aware of these challenges to imperial authority and responded in the way that many others of her time did, that is by a growing sense of imperial responsibility in bettering the lives of her Indian counterparts. For the most part, due to gender constraints, the women of the Raj focused this

authority on Indian women. British women conveyed to their readers the apparently childlike nature of Indian women and, in this way, implied a need for their civilising influence as exemplary wives and mothers. Lady Dufferin's projects like the Female Medical Aid Fund allowed Englishwomen entry into areas of Indian homes otherwise unknown to them. She also displayed genuine sympathy for Indian women and followed the Queen's task of allowing Indian women access to better healthcare with enthusiasm.

The park at Barrackpore was used by Hariot Dufferin to set up picnics and treats for her charitable ventures. Thus she describes how she was in a hurry to reach Government House as 'I had a school feast to see after. Rachel and I went up in the launch, and lunched under the banian-tree, and then soon after four the children began to arrive. . . it contains the most delightful infant of four years that I ever saw. She is such a pretty thing, with a brown skin, such white teeth, pretty brown eyes, and short black hair...she clung to Rachel or me all the day, chattered away in her unknown tongue, played games most merrily, and tied up a quantity of sweets in the corner of her muslin to take home to her mother...'[11]

The tea was very English including chocolate, jelly, ice and bonbons, plum, sponge and seed cakes, while the pensioners who came in later were given beer and meat. Elephant rides were organized for the guests and no one could foresee that the *hathikhana* was getting to be an expensive upkeep and would be done away with ten years later. The Europeans who came from the neighbouring cantonment were 'very grand and dull.'[12]

The guest list had always been a problem for the Governors General from its early days. There had frequently been misgivings about the intermixing of the civil and the military and whether inviting the military officers and their wives from the cantonment would risk offending the swells from Calcutta society, including members of the peerage, who had come as guests. By 1885 this problem was over as the house was more of a weekend retreat rather than a mainline entertainment venue. So the soldiers and their wives came and provided a much needed diversion for the charity parties that Hariot Dufferin set up. Indeed the military presence provided glamour and when the band struck up tunes and the soldier's wives danced to the music, there was much excitement amongst the poor converts 'their performance in that line helping to amuse the little ones.'[13]

Unlike other memsahibs who hated the climate and couldn't adjust to the heat, Hariot took up the challenge. 'Directly after lunch, despite of all Indian rules and regulations, we began to walk about, and we walked the whole afternoon, visiting first a temple in the grounds erected 'to the Memory of

the Brave'. Then we looked at the Flagstaff Bungalow, and made our way over to a place where elephants were to be seen...on our way back we explored the plant-houses and the garden, then had tea on the verandah, and started off on a still longer walk to visit a Hindu temple... we could not enter the sacred precincts but from outside we were allowed to peep at the shrine, where under a silver canopy a metal goddess sits, a crown on her head and a plate of rice in her hand...'[14]

Lord Dufferin had come to India at a crucial period in political history, when his predecessor Lord Ripon had attempted a policy of reform. Indians waited to see whether there would be a return of Ripon's liberal policies or a continuation of the arch-Imperialist attitude of Lord Lytton. Dufferin attempted to maintain a neutral outlook on all and use his charm and social diplomacy to calm and placate. In striking contrast to the attitude of her predecessors, Hariot Dufferin too tried to display an outward tolerance of the colonized and to present a more meaningful picture of life in India as well as of the 'natives'. This is seen in her journal entries.

From March the Dufferins moved on to the customary annual migration up to the north, passing through Allahabad to Lahore, Rawalpindi, and finally Simla. In 1886 they journeyed to Burma in the wake of the British accession of the upper Pegu in what has been described as the most unnecessary annexation in India: 'the Burma government constituted no security threat to India, the potential trade with China was negligible, Burmans did not acquiesce in the abolition of the royal court, the glory-hunt by ambitious army officers turned sour.'[15] For Lady Dufferin the visit to Mandalay was connected with her ambitious project of the new Viceregal Lodge in Simla to which she contributed both layout as well as design. In her journal she describes how the prizes of war would enable her to carry back trophies for her imperial palaces, the carpets and chandeliers for the new Government House at Simla and two Siamese mirrors for the Calcutta house. Volume 1 of the journal ends with a picturesque description of their return to Calcutta after a long departure: 'For many years Viceroys have arrived at a railway station, but in old times when they came by sea they used to disembark at Prinsep's Ghat, and on this occasion we did so too. The mise-en-scene is very superior to that of the station; here a magnificent river, filled with splendid ships, all dressed with flags, and every variety of boat and launch flying about, Calcutta itself on either bank, and the ghat covered with red cloth, flags, and smart spectators. We went ashore at 5.30, and were met by the great officials in their best uniforms, and by Blanche in her best gown, and we walked up the crimson path-way, speaking to people as we went along, and treading upon flowers that were thrown at our feet.'[16] The remainder of their stay in India was taken up by visits to other parts of India as well as the customary summer residence in Simla where the new Viceregal Lodge had been built.

In 1888 the Dufferins left India forever. Lord Dufferin died in 1900 after serving as Ambassador in Rome and France. Hariot Dufferin lived long, perhaps too long. When she died in 1936 aged 93 she had seen the deaths of all her four sons. Though her spirit was unflagging till the end, one wonders if she remembered Barrackpore as a distant memory of sunlight and laughter at a time when tragedy had not clouded her own life. Calcutta, like Barrackpore, had been home and yet not quite so. Part of the picturesque and the visual pleasure of the scene was linked to the detached perspective of the traveller who would soon, when the five years were up, return to the familiar sights of home. Yet while the exotic escapade was in progress, Hariot Dufferin enjoyed it with vigour and an appetite for adventure.

NOTES

1. Agnew, Eadaoin. 2017. Imperial Women Writers in Victorian India: Representing Colonial Life, 1850-1910. Springer.
2. Marchioness of Dufferin & Ava, Hariot. 1890. Our Viceregal Life in India: Selections From My Journal 1884-1888. John Murray.
3. Ibid.
4. Ibid.
5. Ibid.
6. Ibid.
7. Ibid.
8. Ibid.
9. Ibid.
10. Ibid.
11. Ibid.
12. Ibid.
13. Ibid.
14. Ibid.
15. Cady, John. 1973. 'Review of the Pagoda War – Lord Dufferin and the Fall of the Kingdom of Ava 1885-86 by A.T. Stewart' Pacific Affairs Vol 46 No 3. University of British Columbia.
16. Marchioness of Dufferin & Ava, Hariot.

CHAPTER TEN
HAWKS AND KITES

"

"Christmas Eve was spent peacefully at Barrackpore,
and the family lunched by themselves
under the banyan tree"

The Fishing Fleet
Husband-Hunting in the Raj
Anne de Courcy

"

After the Dufferins returned to England, they were succeeded by Lord Lansdowne and Lord Elgin. Lansdowne's tenure has been described as a feeble one in which the Viceroyalty had 'no sense of mission, certainly no appreciation of the poetry of his high office.'[1] However it would be unfair to pass such a sweeping judgement without considering that his tenure marked the demarcation of the Indo-Afghan border, popularly known as the Durand Line. Most of his time and energy was spent in solving the border problem. Fittingly, a hill station called Lansdowne survives till today and serves as a quick getaway for tired Delhites. In Barrackpore, Government House continued its status as a retreat. Photographs graciously made available to the authors of this book by the executors of the Lansdowne legacy show the Viceroy's family and friends in relaxed informality under the shade of the banyan tree, away from the structured Viceregal entertainments of Calcutta. We get a sense that Barrackpore Park was a private place where the privileged official world close to the Viceroy could picnic in the gardens and have a spot of fun. The court etiquettes of Calcutta were kept at a distance, but strict boundaries of racial exclusion continued to be maintained. The Indians in the photographs stand stiff and sober, silent servants and attendants, providing a backdrop to the poses of Viceregal informality.

Lansdowne's successor was Lord Elgin, son of the Viceroy who had died at Dharamshala. Elgin has

Lunch under the Banyan Tree, Barrackpore
© The Trustees of the Bowood Collection

been described by the same writer as being 'The Great Ornamental.' Weak and ineffective, his tenure was also marked by a terrible famine that laid waste to large parts of India.

Lord Elgin's wife was frequently ill, with headaches, insomnia and the rigours of confinement. A child was born to them while Elgin was Viceroy. Their eldest daughter Lady Elisabeth Bruce was seventeen when her father became Viceroy. In her mother's absence she shouldered much of the responsibilities of a Vicereine. Bessie, as she was better known, enjoyed India as well as Barrackpore and her impressions are recorded in a diary which, though still in a private collection, give glimpses of happy times spent at Government House, Barrackpore. Bessie mentions weekend parties and guests including a certain 'Mr. Churchill. . . short, with reddish hair and face, blue eyes—and some of his father's characteristics.'[2] Few remember that the young Winston Churchill who was serving the British army in the North West of India had once stayed at Barrackpore during the Elgins' time.

Bessie had met her future husband Henry Babington Smith in India and shared endearing moments with him at the Park. In Bessie's diary, we find brief glimpses of Barrackpore, of Christmas Eve meals under the banyan tree with the hawks and kites growing tame enough to carry off H.E's beef 'just

Elisabeth Babington Smith and Daughters
© National Portrait Gallery

as it was being put on the table; after which he ordered men with sticks to stand near to guard the table and stove.'[3] On one of her last visits there, 'the stars were sparkling and the fireflies shone among the dark trees... I wished that Virgil had been in India to describe the beautiful nights.'[4] A little later she wrote how 'it was growing dark and Sir George was laid on his long chair underneath a banyan tree on the ramparts... it was curious to sit there and watch the carriages with their lights hurrying along the dusty red road and think that by next year we too shall be part of the past...'[5]

Prophetic enough though she had been, Bessie could not have foretold the sweeping changes that would come to Barrackpore and to Bengal during the time of the next Viceroy Lord Curzon.

It is in Lord Elgin's time that a crucial event occurred at Barrackpore Park that marked out an important

Ronald Ross

moment in the history of world medicine. This was the identification of a mysterious fever which helped the physician Ronald Ross to establish his findings on malaria. It was Ross' work in Calcutta that helped him establish that malaria was transmitted by the anopheles mosquito. As Ross was returning to England to continue his research on tropical diseases, a co-passenger on the voyage out confirmed that visitors at Barrackpore had come down with intermittent bouts of fever with shivering because they were not sleeping under mosquito nets. Here are Ross' own words tracing the outbreak: 'On my voyage home from Calcutta last March, Mr. J. F. Parker, of Messrs. Thacker, Spink, and Co., of Calcutta, and Mrs. Parker, who were travelling in the same vessel with me, volunteered the following statement regarding an outbreak of fever. I cannot answer for the facts, because I was not aware of the case at the time it occurred, and because a letter which I addressed to Calcutta on the subject appears to have miscarried; but Mr. and Mrs. Parker seemed

to be so familiar with the circumstances, and to be so certain regarding those facts, that I think I may venture to record the case...The 1st Calcutta Company of the Boys' Brigade went out to camp in the month of October, 1898. They were given the use of one of the bungalows in Barrackpore Park, fourteen miles from Calcutta. Barrackpore Park is the estate around Government House at Barrackpore; the bungalow referred to is one occasionally used by the Viceroy's staff, and is a brick built structure, soundly made, containing large rooms, and surrounded by a verandah. The water supply is the same as that of Calcutta. The kitchen is the Viceroy's kitchen. There are some ponds about the park, and the river Hooghly flows close by. The party in camp consisted of three

Winston Churchill in India
© Mark Bence Jones, The Viceroys of India

officers, all young men, and thirteen boys of between 13 and 18 years of age. The officers were Mr. -, the captain, and Mr. - and Mr. -, the two lieutenants. The whole party slept in the bungalow every night for one week, and also ate their meals there. During the week the party lived in the bungalow, the boys did not sleep under mosquito nets because it was feared they would tear them, although the three officers did so. Mr. - (the captain) informed us that mosquitos were very numerous, and that the boys were bitten by them. On the last day of the week a sister of one of the boys visited the camp, and was also bitten so much that her arm swelled; she was present only in the day. All the boys were attacked by malarial fever within a few days after the close of the camp. One died, and several were seriously ill. Three native servants who went with the party were also, to our certain knowledge, taken ill, one, a boy, seriously. The two other servants were lent to the party by ourselves. The little girl just referred to was also attacked the day after her visit. The medical man attending the boys stated that the disease was malarial fever, and this was the disease entered on the death certificate of the one who died, named M. We heard that the boys had repeated attacks of shivering followed by fever. M. was the first attacked (the day after returning), and all the rest were attacked within about ten days.

Moments of leisure under the Banyan Tree
© The Trustees of the Bowood Collection

The three officers (who slept in mosquito nets) remained perfectly well up to February 23rd, 1899, when Mr. and Mrs. Parker left for England. The officers slept every night in the bungalow. A friend of the captain's, Mr. -, also slept in the bungalow one night in a mosquito net, and was not attacked. The food of the whole party was precisely the same. The three native servants, of course, did not sleep under mosquito nets. Thus, out of twenty-one persons concerned, seventeen who did not use mosquito nets were all attacked with fever, while four who did use them all escaped. Mr. and Mrs. Parker have authorised me to publish their names in connection with this case.'[6]

For Barrackpore Park, land of water and flowers, languorous retreat of the Lordsahibs and Ladysahibs, there had always been a sense of Edenic splendour inspite of the sorrows encountered there. Not long after, the rose-beds would be neglected and the house fall to disuse, but till then the birds swooped over the green lawns, the water-lilies bloomed on the shining lakes and the air was thick and warm with the fragrance of rose and honeysuckle.

There was a troubled restlessness in the world beyond, in Calcutta and the rest of India; but at Government House things were exactly the same as they had been fifty years before. Time seemed to stand still and it would still be a decade before the spell would be broken.

NOTES ──

1. Bence-Jones, Mark. 1982. The Viceroys of India. Constable.
2. de Courcy, Anne. 2013. The Fishing Fleet. Windsor.
3. Ibid.
4. Ibid.
5. Ibid.
6. Ross Ronald, 'An Outbreak of Fever Attributed to Mosquitoes', The British Medical Journal, Vol. 2, No. 2012 (Jul. 22, 1899).

CHAPTER ELEVEN

QUIET HOURS FOR WORK

❝

"Nearly all visitors to Calcutta, and the majority of European residence, have been up the river to this country retreat of the Governor General, have wandered in the bamboo avenues, or perhaps lunched under the shady colonnades of the great banian, have admired the flaming bougainvillea, or played golf in the Park."

British Government in India, The Story of the Viceroys
and Government Houses
George Curzon The Marquis of Kedleston

❞

In October 1925 Lord Curzon's life was closing in upon him. He was politically a nonentity, with King George V choosing Stanley Baldwin over him as British Prime Minister in 1923. Physically, a spine injury which had caused him to wear a steel corset all his adult life was now worse and there were times when he couldn't sleep without laudanum. Emotionally, he was exhausted by financial conflicts with both his daughters Irene and Cynthia, as strong willed as their father, over the provisions of their mother Mary Leiter's will. He was also disillusioned by his second wife Grace

Duggan whom he had married in 1917 and who, like his first wife, had failed to bear him a male heir. Worse still, she had already taken on new lovers and Curzon grew lonelier.

At such a time he went to stay with an old friend at the French Riviera and spent most of his time in his room writing a book on India. He left France in February after a brief period of happiness, tearfully bidding farewell to his host and hostess and telling them that he had not had such a happy holiday since he was a young man. The book that

Mary and George Curzon
© Granger Historical Photo Archive

he had been writing, *British Government in India*, had been finished; he had been checking the proofs of Volume 2 and completing the job of indexing when he died suddenly in London of a severe bladder haemorrhage.

Given that Curzon finished this book in the last few months of his life creates an interesting context. It appears to be not just a narrative of British history in India, an account of the Raj, its legacies, political events and architectural achievements. It also functioned as a lament for a time of glory and renown long past. For a man shackled by failing health and diverse troubles, writing this book enabled him to return to a time when he was in full control, the self assured Viceroy of the largest colonial power in the world. 'Great things are expected of G. as ever. Since the days of Lord Dalhousie there have been good but not great Viceroys and the whole of India has awakened to the belief that G. will do great things,'[1] Mary Curzon had written in a letter home. Curzon had himself carried on with his tumultuous tenure of Viceroy sustained by a firm belief in his own suitability for the task at hand. His tenure had begun in triumph, 'I never saw such crowds as there were in the streets...we bowed & bowed & all cheered & cheered and it was a marvellous sight,'[2] but had ended in acrimony and a humiliating return: 'We have had a very exciting week, welcomed by everyone but the ex-Cabinet whose hostility & venom pursues George.'[3]

Throughout the book, as Curzon meticulously details the lives of the men who created India, there is an undercurrent of melancholy at the colonial power's present state, rife with uprisings against the British and the strident demands for self governance. And so Curzon looks back to the past, personal as well as colonial, and recreates the pomp and grandeur, the levees, dances, official dinners and parties, the princes in their diamonds and pearls, himself in regalia in the *Delhi Durbar* of 1902, with its parades, polos, parties and the wonderful *tamasha* that the event was designed to be. As had happened earlier Curzon's time also had an outward pageantry which covered the murkiness of the inner administration that had caused a mercantile company to build up an Empire.

In a way Curzon was a romantic. In his youth, carefully preparing himself for a career in India, he had travelled to far flung places to acclimatise himself to the East, to Afghanistan and Persia, to Tashkent and Samarqand. It is said that he was a

Curzon at Aden, 1898
© Qatar National Library

man of overpowering ambition who ran India with the 'Napoleon complex', running an empire without delegation of powers, single-handedly and purposefully. But it could also be that he felt the pull of the East, with its palaces and finery. He had a passion for majestic architecture, fine old houses and castles. In 1911 he had bought the 15th century Tattershall Castle in Lincolnshire and restored it. Later he also restored Bodiam Castle in Sussex and presented both of them to the National Trust in Britain. In India he had carried out extensive restorations at the Taj Mahal and gifted a huge copper and bronze chandelier to it in 1908, to be kept near the mausoleum. In England he had inherited, bought or leased five houses: Kedleston Manor, 1 Carlton House Terrace, Hackwood Park

in Hampshire, Montacute House in Somerset, Naldera Villa at Broadstairs beside the two castles already mentioned.

It thus comes as no surprise that while in India, Government House Barrackpore was singled out for attention, its history lovingly detailed and the house put to use more frequently than any of his immediate predecessors. For the first time in many years Barrackpore was actually loved more than Simla. Though the mandatory move in summer had to be made to escape the heat, in Simla he preferred camping at Naldera rather than at the polished perfection of the Viceregal Lodge on Observatory Hill or even The Retreat at Mashobra, purchased by Lord Elgin. His youngest daughter Alexandra was

Curzon at Aden on the way to India
© Qatar National Library

conceived at Naldera and named Alexandra Naldera Curzon, nicknamed Baba from *Missy Baba* or little one, the standard name by which Indian servants would call the sahib's daughter.

Mary Curzon's letters describe the Viceroy's life in detail. In Calcutta, Government House was the scene of hectic socialising. In 1899, in January and February the Curzons had presided over one State Ball for 1600, a State Evening Party for 1500, a Garden Party, smaller balls for about 600 guests, official dinners for about a 100 and informal evening dances. In between these there were visits to the races where 'we drove up the course in State like Ascot, got out and went to the Royal box from which we looked at the racing & were stared at the whole afternoon.'[4]

In contrast Barrackpore, where they spent their weekends, was a place for private recreation and family time, where 'George gets quiet hours for work and I get plenty of time for the children, who are flourishing.'[5]

There was the luxuriant life reminiscent of royalty: 'Everyone has a quantity of attendants and each of these has his special occupation and his caste only permits him to do that one. One man heats your bathwater, another brings it & a third pours it into the tub. A fourth empties it and he being quite low caste does the objectionable things which no drains necessitate. Quite a different lot wait on you at breakfast and there is a waiter for every person at table... George and I each have a high caste attendant who sits outside our doors & attends us wherever we go. My swell's name is Ramdas, and whenever we drive out he sits up in the rumble behind the Great barouche & behind him stands a Syce–two postillions in front two outriders, eight bodyguards & one officer and a policeman so it takes eighteen people beside the ADC in the carriage to take a Viceroy out.'[6]

Barrackpore was the one place where Mary Curzon had her husband all to herself, for brief moments of domestic bliss. They had luncheon and tea under the enormous banyan tree, 'and as huge kites swoop down and carry off all the food on your plate native servants stand about with great sticks wh (sic) they wave at them. Monday morning we came back to Calcutta by launch, all–especially Irene–having loved our Sunday, and rested for all our labours this week.'[7]

From March the gaiety moved to Simla. The pattern followed for the rest of their stay in India as it had for the Viceroys who had gone before - Calcutta in winter, Barrackpore over the weekends, relief from the heat at Simla in summer. In future years Mary took to retreating in stages, first by withdrawing to Barrackpore when Calcutta got oppressive, then retreating to Darjeeling or Nainital as an intermediate measure and finally retiring to Simla. Mary often sent her children to Darjeeling early in the year with their nurses and attendants to keep them away from the blistering heat of Calcutta.

In recent times there has been a resurgence of interest in Curzon, not as the arrogant and indefatigable devotee of imperial pomp, might and grandeur but as someone who cared for and created a remembered past for the British in India. The 1857 Revolt had begun at Barrackpore, as had a previous rebellion in the time of Lord Amherst.

Barrackpore was thus a significant milestone in the history of British India, like the battle at Plassey and the Black Hole tragedy in Calcutta. In each area Curzon created appropriate memoralisations. In Plassey he had the positions of the various forces on the battlefield marked out by small pillars and erected an obelisk, designed by himself, on the highest point of the field. In Calcutta he carefully marked out the position of the Black Hole, the room in the Old Fort where Siraj-ud-daullah had supposedly murdered 123 English men, women and children by suffocating them. He also installed a memorial to the tragedy, the original built by Holwell having been destroyed in 1821.[8] The Victoria Memorial was the climax of this process: the creation of an abiding British legacy as well as a museum enshrining the past through an imposing monument, honouring Britain's iconic Queen. The Victoria Memorial began its existence as a timeless signifier of a particular past but was appropriated by the colonised nation itself as a

Curzon on the way to India, 1898
© Qatar National Library

suitable marker for a newly constituted nationalist identity. Today, Curzon's monument is to Calcutta what the Big Ben is to London, its most loved landmark and the city's representative symbol. In the process it has acquired an identity of its own where colonialism and nationalism have merged.

In Barrackpore, Curzon beautified where he could, putting in comfortable armchairs, converting the vegetable garden into a rose garden from where roses could be sent to the Calcutta house for decorations. There were climbing roses raised on a pergola, the first such at Barrackpore. A billiard table was carried to the House from Government House, Calcutta and new *shamianas* were draped under the banyan tree. The long tank or Moti Jheel was turfed to prevent mosquitoes from breeding. As in the time of Lord Lansdowne, golf was allowed

Lord and Lady Curzon on an elephant, 1903
© Alamy Stock Photo

to be played in the Park, picnics permitted and when the Viceroy was away the park and gardens were thrown open to the public.

Mary Curzon died in July 1906 of a heart attack when she was thirty-six. Only a few months before Curzon, in a terrible quarrel with General Kitchener over questions of administrative control, had resigned and returned to England. The continuous entertaining and the strenuous travelling across the length and breadth of India, where they visited forty native states, as also the strain of the magnificent *Delhi Durbar* of 1902 had left their mark on the frail Vicereine. So too had her futile efforts at bearing a son and her illness at London had broken her down. In December 1901, on the eve of the *Durbar* she wrote to Curzon from Dehradun an ominous letter : 'Every bit of my vitality has gone, and I am iller than I have ever been and simply can't get back to life somehow... I believe absolutely in my power of 'coming up to time' or answering my ring, as an actor does. Some day, though, the bell will go and I shall not appear, as India, I know, slowly but surely murders women.'9

In the end, twenty years or so after her death, through a difficult second marriage, unsuccessful liaisons, and tottering on the brink of extinction, Curzon returned to the days of his youth and the days of his glory in his historical reconstruction of Barrackpore. In a beautifully worded tribute he describes how 'In later days the charm of the place to an overworked man lay not merely in the enjoyment of its restful beauties - though rest there was little, my sojourns at Barrackpore being days of accumulated arrears and unending files - but in the journeys up and down the river in the twilight of a Saturday evening, or in the dewy radiance of

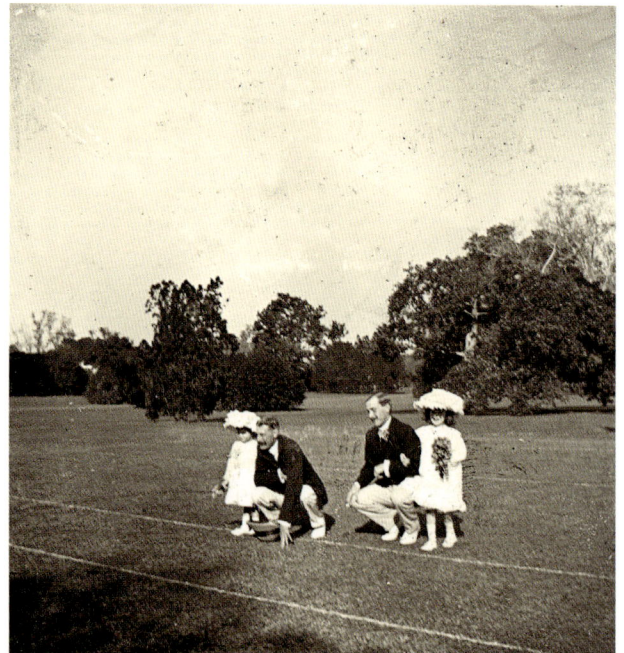

Mary Curzon with her daughters Irene, Cynthia or Cimmie and Alexandra or Baba enjoying Barrackpore Park
Curzon Collection
© British Library Board

a Monday morning. Motors had not yet invaded Calcutta, and a small steam launch was the means of transport. To leave the city in the late afternoon and, after tea on the deck, to lie in a lounge chair and watch the changing panorama of the river banks as they flew by - the thick fringe of the vegetation and the feathery palm tops; the smoke of the native villages; the white clad figures moving up and down the dilapidated ghats; the glare of the electric light suddenly switched on in some great jute mill... and then, when light had vanished and all was swathed in shadow, to land by the glimmering tomb of Lady Canning, and to walk up the gravelled terrace to Barrackpore House, the hand-borne

Government House Barrackpore, 1905-1906
© Queen Mary's Visiting Book, Royal Collection Trust

lanterns twinkling in the darkness ahead - these were sensations that can never be forgotten.'[10]

Curzon regarded Calcutta as a British city and called it 'a great graveyard of memories'– a vast layered metropolis of colonial dreams. For him Calcutta was never Kipling's 'city of dreadful night', indeed he felt Kipling's comments outrageously malicious. It was instead the city of Macaulay and Thackeray, of Rose Aylmer, of the large elegant *maidan* and the broad Hooghly with its masted ships. He was stiffly opposed to the shifting of the capital to Delhi.

While Government House, Calcutta was modelled on his own house at Kedleston, the house at Barrackpore Park may have reminded him of the sweeping meadows and rolling parklands of home. Perhaps it is time that Bengal forgives him for the partition of 1905 and remembers him as a heritage conservationist.

Certainly Jawaharlal Nehru did so! 'After every other Viceroy has been forgotten, Curzon will be remembered because he restored all that was beautiful in India.'[11] said Nehru. The time has come to agree.

Statue of Curzon in front of the Victoria Memorial Hall, Calcutta
© Sushen Mitra

Victoria Memorial Hall, Calcutta
© Sushen Mitra

Lord Kitchener, Lord Curzon and the Duke of Connaught walking past Indian cavalry
© Royal Collection Trust

NOTES

1. Lady Curzon, Mary and Nicholson, Nigel. 1986. Lady Curzon's India: Letters of a Vicereine. Olympic Marketing Corp. Edited by John Bradley.
2. Ibid.
3. Ibid.
4. Ibid.
5. Ibid.
6. Ibid.
7. Ibid.
8. Metcalfe, T.R. 2005. Forging the Raj: Essays on British India in the Heyday of Empire. Oxford University Press.
9. Lady Curzon, Mary and Nicholson, Nigel.
10. K.G, The Marquis Curzon of Kedleston. 1925. British Government in India: The Story of the Viceroys and Government Houses. Cassel and Company Ltd.
11. Rose, Kenneth, 2011. Superior Person : A Portrait of Curzon and His Circle in Late Victorian England. Phoenix

CHAPTER TWELVE

SWAN SONG

"

*"We breakfasted, as usual, under the banyan tree, and
the whole party went to church........Otherwise sitting
under the shamianas with our tropical surroundings,
we could hardly believe that it was Christmas Day....."*

Vicereine: The Indian Journal of Mary Minto
Edited by Anabel Loyd

"

'By means of the King's influence it has now been settled that George Curzon shall receive the Prince and Princess at Bombay, and that I shall arrive thereafter. Their Royal Highnesses have started on their tour. George Curzon will then receive me and sail at once for home, and I shall go straight on to Calcutta and receive the Prince and Princess there at the end of the year.'[1]

Gilbert Elliot Murray, the fourth Earl of Minto, former Governor of Canada, fondly called Rolly by his intimates, arrived in India in 1905 under trying circumstances. The Curzon resignation had coincided with the Prince and Princess of Wales' tour of India (later King George V and Queen Mary) and laborious questions remained as to who would receive them – the outgoing or the incoming Viceroy. In the end tact prevailed and it is one of the cornerstones of Lord Minto's rule that with persuasion and as much discretion as possible in a land boiling with anger against the Raj, he managed to soothe the feathers which Lord Curzon had stormily ruffled and navigate his tenure without endless controversy. 'Minto might have been chosen for the reason that he was in every respect the opposite of his predecessor'[2] said Mark Bence-Jones, before outlining their differences.

Both Curzon and Minto had been friends at college and had been part of the avant garde London set.

Mary Minto & Lord Minto at Barrackpore

Yet in personality they were very different, and Minto's unfazed equanimity contrasts with Curzon's tempestuous outlook.

But if there was one point of absolute agreement it was their common love for Barrackpore Park. Just as Curzon adored his weekend retreat, so too did Minto. Fortunately for us Mary Minto, the new Vicereine, was of more robust health than her predecessor and namesake and also had a passion for photography, so that many of the early 20th century attractions of Barrackpore have been preserved for posterity in the many photographs taken on her Kodak as she swung down the paths and gardens of Government House.

On Saturday the 25th of November 1905, almost a hundred years after the 1st Earl of Minto had made his visit, the Mintos came to Barrackpore. The *Soonamookie* was now obsolete with the introduction of new steam launches and the Mintos travelled by the *Maud*, quickly and effortlessly landing at the ghat, past the bamboo avenue planted by Lady Ripon to the main house and grounds. The unanimous opinion was that it was lovely. The Vicereine felt herself to be in a fairy land, with the glorious garden, the lush trees and grass parkland stretching for miles along the riverbank. The Viceroy, in a letter to Lord Morley describes how 'the large tropical garden is ablaze with bougainvillea and blue morning glory convolvulus, and is surrounded by an extensive English-looking park with golf links and tennis courts. The heat-haze shimmers across the wide grassy glades which lead down to the river Hooghly; there is nothing in Barrackpore to disturb the peace except the occasional shouts of the drivers to their bullocks drawing their creaking carts slowly round the garden, to pick up tiny heaps of dead leaves from the lawns which the *malis* (gardeners) sweep clean as a billiard table. A bamboo avenue leads from the river to the large square house, full of old Chippendale furniture, where the Viceroy and his family live. A picture of Warren Hastings hangs in the drawing-room, looking down on the descendants of his own severe critic, the Ist Lord Minto...During an evening ride one can canter for miles down sandy lanes between bamboo avenues, passing many small villages with picturesque groups of natives resting outside their houses after the day's work. Naked brown children with large wondering eyes play about; the sun is setting; the Monkey-God sits under his shelter contemplating the water-tank over which he presides; the smell of the evening fires permeates the air, and one rides home past the barracks where in 1857 the first sign of Revolt amongst the native troops appeared.'[3]

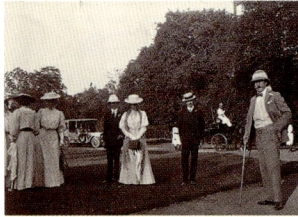

DUKE AND DUCHESS OF CONNAUGHT AT THE BOTANICAL GARDENS.   H. H. SEINDIO HIS EXCELLENCY PRINCESS AT TOLLYGUNGE   DUCHESS OF CONNAUGHT   H. H.   AFTER LUNCHEON AT BARRACKPORE

Captain
Holden, the popular commandant of the Viceroy's Bodyguard, won the fine double event of the big cup and the pony-chase cup, Mrs. Lamond Walker the Ladies' Cup, Dr. Forsyth the Heavy Weight Cup, and Mr. Ballantyne the Average Cup. And so ends the most delightful feature of our cold weather-season. It has been prolific in accidents, but luckily none of them have been serious, and it has afforded us, for the first time on record, the opportunity of numbering among the field a Viceroy, his wife, daughters, and son.

BACK ROW :—Lady Ruby. Count Wedell. Lady Violet. Capt. Fitzgerald. Miss Janet D. Smith. Countess Wedell. Col. D. Smith. Mrs. Adam. Mrs. Pelly. Col. Crooke-Lawless. Miss Smith. Gent. J. Maxwell. Mrs. Crooke-Lawless. Major Feilding.
MIDDLE ROW :—Princess Patricia. Lord Kitchener. Duchess of Connaught. The Viceroy. Duke of Connaught. Her Excellency. Hon. E. Elliot. General Negrier.
FRONT ROW :—Colonel Adam. Captain Mackenzie. Major Brooke. Captain Elgee. Maharaja Scindia. Captain Miles Ponsonby. Lady Eileen Elliot. Capt. Webber. Capt. Bulkeley.

Barrackpore Park
© Timothy Melgund, 7th Earl of Minto

They visited the cenotaph built by the first Lord Minto in what one presumes was a proud moment for the new Viceroy. Then they sat down for the customary lunch beneath the banyan tree with servants chasing the kites away as they swooped down for the meat. This was followed by a visit to the cantonment church.

Christmas was spent at Barrackpore. In 1905 Lady Minto describes the Orientalised church decorations, with their poinsettia, bougainvillea, marigolds and nasturtiums. Though the lunches and dinners had turkey, mince pies and plum puddings, home could

not always be successfully recreated and instead of the snowy paths of home there was the pleasant heat of Calcutta. Fireside frolic was replaced by conjurers on the lawn, with rupee coins coming out of oranges and threaded rings on sticks 'which had never left the Viceroy's hands.'[4]

In 1906 modernisation won again as they motored down to Barrackpore on the new 6 cylinder Napier. Electricity had been installed and a teak floor laid out in the drawing room which was a sprung floor to facilitate dancing. The parties included games and uproarious finales with 'crackers being pulled

W. and Mrs. Ian Malcolm.

Eileen. Major Fielding. Lord F. Scott. Ruby.

Lord and Lady Minto have not been long in making the acquaintance of their pleasant country-house at Barrackpore, where the Viceregal party is accustomed to lead the simple life from Saturday to Monday. The house is not more than an unpretentious bungalow, but it is prettily placed in a beautiful park full of grand old trees. There are also nice golf links, which should appeal to our Scottish Viceroy. Another interesting survival of olden times is the building known as Honeymoon Lodge, which, according to popular belief, is kept up solely for the benefit of any member of the Staff who may be tempted to take a sudden plunge into the matrimonial estate.

From my Calcutta correspondent:
"One of the most delightful features of our cold weather is the early morning gallop on the racecourse before the sun has gathered full strength; but few of Viceroys have been known to indulge in this refreshment before labour, so it the more pleasant for us to see our new Ruler riding with his daughters the track, and inspecting with a critical eye the gallops of the racehorses. Minto is so great a lover of horses and has such a neat seat in the saddle that is now no occasion for a remonstrance on the subject of a too cautious prefe for the safety of a carriage, such as once caused the barring of the doors of Go ment House to a certain well-known sporting journalist and his family, in the of Lord Elgin.

Snake Charmers.

Christmas Day at Barrackpore. 1905.

Barrackpore Park
© Timothy Melgund, 7th Earl of Minto

at dessert,'[5] the guest list was varied but invariably had Lord Kitchener of Khartoum, the Commander-in-Chief as an enthusiastic dancer.

Always present, however, was the fear of the East and what it could do to the sahib; in the tomb of Lady Canning which they passed to and fro in their daily rambles lay a mute reminder of the sufferings that Empire could bring. There was also a new restlessness amongst the Indians which the British privately conceded to be hints that their days were numbered. In a letter from Lord Morley to Minto in August 1907 he admitted to 'realize how intensely artificial and unnatural is our mighty Raj, and it sets one wondering whether it can possibly last. It surely cannot, and our only business is to do what we can to make the next transition, whatever it may turn out to be.'[6]

The same year Lady Minto described how 'Every time Minto drove through the crowded part of the city on his way to Barrackpore, the Staff told me, they were in agonies. Five times stones were thrown at the car, and on one occasion a huge brick splintered the window, missing Minto's head by an inch, and yet they didn't dare pause for fear a bomb

Barrackpore Park
© Timothy Melgund, 7th Earl of Minto

might be placed in front of the car while they were waiting.'⁷

Meanwhile life went on at Barrackpore. The Prince and Princess of Wales came and went and Lady Minto recorded how 700 men had been employed in painting, cleaning and preparing the house for the Royal visit.

Later, the Amir of Afghanistan Habibullah spent an exciting weekend in February 1907, the account of which is surely one of the most hilarious in Lady Minto's journal. The 'tubby and flirtatious' Amir played croquet with the Viceroy's eldest daughter

Eileen, invited himself to a State Ball in Calcutta, bestowed gifts on pretty women and in spite of broad hints, would not go away. He had been invited with the aim of creating an useful ally, 'In the Amir we have a neighbour whose friendship is absolutely necessary to us in its connection with the frontier tribes and Mahommedan influence, a neighbour whom it would be disastrous to fall foul of, for both Afghanistan and the frontier tribes are now infinitely stronger than they have ever been before, whilst the Mahommedan influence, of which the Amir is, in the North of India, a dominating representative, is becoming more and more accentuated, whilst perhaps most important

Barrackpore Park
© Timothy Melgund, 7th Earl of Minto

of all is the effect Japanese successes have produced upon the Eastern mind in the direction that European Armies, as represented by Russia, are not invincible, and that the military forces of Afghanistan need no longer fear to cross bayonets with Russian outposts.'[8] Here is Kipling's Great Game and the Amir had to be placated for his part in it, though none could have foreseen the consequences.

In 1907 Minto wrote despairingly to Morley that 'The Amir is still with us! These words can hardly convey what they mean to me! Lady Minto and I are at the last stages of exhaustion! He fills up every one's spare moment. He came down to Barrackpore on Sunday for luncheon, after which I had hoped for an afternoon to myself, but was unable to leave him. He then got involved in a game of croquet with my daughters, and finally remained till dark. He has shot clay pigeons with me, though, for international reasons, I thought it wiser to divest the amusement of the conditions of a match! The worst of it is he won't go away, and now, though every one was sworn to secrecy, he has discovered that our State Ball is on Friday and insists on remaining for that. A horrible rumour reached me

Barrackpore
© Timothy Melgund, 7th Earl of Minto

this morning that he wants to stay for the Races on Saturday, but I have told McMahon that he absolutely must insist on his leaving as His Majesty's Ships are specially awaiting his arrival at Bombay, where there is a naval programme which he cannot neglect. He is simply irrepressible...'9

Mary Minto's journal reiterates the feeling that there was always something special about Barrackpore. Indeed it seems to have been the real home, a private house where one could indulge oneself away from the formalities of Calcutta. In between the fascinating accounts of pigsticking, *zenana* parties, hospital visits and charity fetes there

Fountain designed by Sir John Marshall. Erected in Barrackpore Garden Nov. 1910.

m.m.

m.m. with Creepy & Crawley. Barrackpore

Barrackpore
© Timothy Melgund, 7th Earl of Minto

was always the blessed quiet of the 'usual Sundays'[10] at the Park.

In 1907 the Vicereine bought fresh furnishings in London for the three houses under her special care at Simla, Calcutta and Barrackpore. The furniture was changed, gay coverings of pink and green silk and tapestry provided for armchairs and sofas. Carpets were bought for the rooms and *shamianas* for the banyan tree. In photographs taken at this time we see the Viceroy playing golf with *dhoti* clad caddies as Dandy their terrier frolicked in the background. The jackals were still there, causing much excitement to Dandy and adding 'greatly to his enjoyment of life'[11] on the sweeping grounds of Barrackpore House.

In 1909, Lord Minto's youngest daughter Violet married Charles Petty - Fitzmaurice who was Lord Lansdowne's son and after the ceremony in Calcutta they drove off to Barrackpore. In 1910 when her sister Louisa came for a visit the Vicereine drove down to Barrackpore for 'a completely undisturbed afternoon.'[12] It was not unknown to see Mary Minto and her family take a drive down the nearby villages, perhaps on dogcarts pulled by the ponies Creepy and Crawley, driving amongst the Indian settlements, photographing the villagers, even visiting temples of 'a gigantic pink God with a monkey face sitting on a platform'[13] and listening to legends of Rama and Ravana.

The Mintos were in India at a time when the rising tide of nationalism was making itself felt. This was the era of the Extremists and Curzon's Partition politics had tempers running high. There are references in Minto's letters, as well as in Mary Minto's Journal entries, of bombs being thrown at them, of Tilak's transportation to Mandalay, of riots and unrest, all of which make the balmy evenings at Barrackpore even more welcome.

Under the circumstances the Vicereine did her best to reach out to the people and understand the fast paced change around her. Her journal speaks of covert meetings with Annie Besant and Margaret Noble, of trips to Kalighat and Dakshineswar, of treading the maze of lanes of North Calcutta which no Vicereine had ever done before and attending *purdah* parties for native women, where she allowed herself to be dressed up as an Indian bride. Of course she still interacted with the swells of Indian society, and her friends included Cornelia Sorabjee, the Maharanis of Cooch Behar, Mayurbhanj and Burdwan but somewhere a start had been made.

When the time came to depart from India the Viceroy and Lady Minto said goodbye to their vast establishment at Government House, Calcutta. All their servants and *khitmatgars* were given presents

Mary Minto
© Timothy Melgund, 7th Earl of Minto

The pink God with the monkey face
Temple near Barrackpore Park
© Sushen Mitra

and the Vicereine noted, in her journal, the names of many devoted staff like Ram Das, Rumbully, Mahommed Khan and Taher Das. For her predecessors they had been nameless, existing like shadowy creatures simply to serve but Mary Minto was sensitised enough to give them a shape and a form in her journal.

In 1909 a wistful note creeps into Mary Minto's journal. The time had come to return to England and so she planned a new garden to leave behind, with a lovely fountain in the middle. The Minto Fountain, as it was known, was designed by Lady Minto and was to be carved in grey stone, with an estimated cost of two thousand rupees. It was to be installed at the Curzon Minto Rose garden but engineering difficulties got in the way. By this time their departure was imminent and Lady Minto approved of the fountain to be set up in another spot known as the Minto Flower Garden near the Aviary Pond. The basin of the fountain was big enough for the 2nd Earl of Lytton, Governor of Bengal in 1922, to use as a plunge pool.

On her birthday on the 13th of November, 1910, Mary Minto was back at Barrackpore, enjoying the perfect temperature and the moon which lighted up the whole river. She formally inaugurated the Minto fountain which remained her parting gift to Barrackpore Park.

A week later she bade good bye saying 'I think my happiest times in India have been spent at Barrackpore and I am glad to have had one more peaceful day there.'[14] For someone who had full enjoyment of the sights and sounds of India, this was a tremendous tribute.

Unfortunately for Government House, Barrackpore it would also be its last.

NOTES

1. Countess of Minto, Mary. 1934. India, Minto and Morley, 1905-1910; Compiled From the Correspondence of the Viceroy and the Secretary of State. Macmillan.
2. Bence-Jones, Mark. 1982. The Viceroys of India. Constable.
3. Countess of Minto, Mary.
4. Loyd, Anabel D. 2017. Vicereine: The Indian Journal of Mary, Countess of Minto. Academic Foundation.
5. Ibid.
6. Countess of Minto, Mary.
7. Loyd, Anabel D.
8. Countess of Minto, Mary.
9. Ibid.
10. Loyd, Anabel D.
11. Ibid.
12. Ibid.
13. Ibid.
14. Ibid.

CHAPTER THIRTEEN

A WORLD IN TURMOIL

"

"Thus we see that the House, the gardens and in fact the whole of the Barrackpore Estate, have passed through a period of considerable progress... and while unparalleled unrest is raging through the length and breadth of the whole country, this blessed spot, so close to the vortex of disturbances, maintains an atmosphere of absolute peace and tranquility"

History of Barrackpore Park
AC Paul

"

In November 1910 Lord Hardinge of Penshurst arrived in India as its new Viceroy. Much of his tenure would be taken up with the business of shifting India's capital from Calcutta to Delhi. Perhaps this shift was the natural culmination of the British distrust of the Bengali Baboo as being politically conscious and incendiary. Certainly the outbreak of violence in the aftermath of the Bengal partition was an important factor in the decision.

The new King George V made the announcement in his *Durbar* of 1911 and twenty years later the

new Capital was formally inaugurated by Lord Irwin. Official correspondences and government dispatches of this period offer close glimpses of the mood in British circles at the unexpected event of the transfer of capital. Reactions varied from racial typecasting of Bengalis as being rebellious and untrustworthy to religious divisiveness and the creation of tropes of the loyal Muslim and the subversive Hindu.

There was also, however, regret at the shift amidst a general feeling of nostalgia for Calcutta's British

Lord Hardinge

would welcome this change. Calcutta, with its century and a half of British government would still retain its illustrious past as 'a perpetual position.'[2]

In reality this vengeful imperial act was a huge blow for Calcutta as the city gradually sank into irrelevance. Bombay had already shaped into a commercial success and now Delhi was to be the political centre! Most Indians shared in their displeasure of the new Viceroy, the Press were vitriolic in their judgement and even Curzon and Minto in England were critical. For Hardinge the move to Delhi therefore became something of a personal challenge: 'He is mad on Delhi at present. I'm afraid we shan't get much of a policy out of him as he can think of little except Delhi'[3] complained the civil servant Sir Spencer Harcourt Butler.

The Hardinges left Government House, Calcutta in March 1912. The house was taken over by the Governor of Bengal while Government House, Barrackpore was retained for Viceregal visits. Before they left, their visits to Barrackpore had been reportedly happy. Lord Hardinge had an additional *shamiana* pitched under a peepal tree, alongside the Great Banyan and was often to be seen seated there 'in the spring of 1911...absorbed in discussing with his colleagues matters of grave importance.'[4]

During Lord Hardinge's time the Viceregal steamer *Maud* met with an accident near the present day Howrah Bridge. A new and bigger launch was pressed into service named *Empress Mary*. This was the launch which carried the King Emperor George V and Queen Mary in 1912 from Calcutta to Barrackpore after the Delhi Durbar.

past. The creation of Lieutenant Governors for Chhotanagpur, Bihar and Orissa was applauded as being a good move because it gave 'a clearer expression of their local individuality.'[1] The hardy law-abiding inhabitants of Bihar, the sanctity of religious traditions amongst the Oriyas and the aboriginal simplicity of the inhabitants of Chhotanagpur were distinguished from the quarrelsome and politically minded Bengalis. The Mohammadans of eastern Bengal, it was felt, would be delighted by the selection of Dacca as the capital of East Bengal and Muslims in general would be rewarded for British loyalty by a hallowing of Mughal Delhi as the imperial capital. Everyone, it was felt,

Lady Hardinge

Bengal and was henceforth listed as a Circuit House in exchange for Belvedere. A contemporary account however maintains that the Governors loved the house and park no less than their Viceregal predecessors.

Lord Carmichael was the first Governor to inherit the Park and declared his intent to spend a large amount of his time there. Accordingly, trees were cut down and the shrubberies thinned so that the cool river breeze could blow inland. A new garden was laid out by Lady Carmichael north of the Ellenborough Terrace and a private golf link was made.

Further alterations were planned, but the house had now been sufficiently downgraded to suffer. Passing from the Viceroy's hands into the Bengal Governor's care, there was never quite enough to help in its maintenance. Moreover, it was wartime and Britain's faltering economy entailed a cutback in funds. There was little money to pay for the upkeep of what had by now become a peripheral piece of property.

Unfortunately for the House, Lady Hardinge died suddenly in 1914 and their son died in World War I. Thereafter Viceregal visits were rare.

In 1919 the Viceroy Lord Chelmsford transferred the Barrackpore House to the Governor of Bengal as his weekend retreat and took over Belvedere, the former residence of the Lieutenant Governor as being more fashionably in the city. Most of the furniture was carried away and distributed amongst the Viceregal lodges.

In 1921, Government House, Barrackpore was transferred to the domain of the Government of

Lord Hardinge did his best by sanctioning sums of money regularly for the use of the estate. The Governors of Bengal did what they could within their limitations. Lord Ronaldshay built a girder bridge to link the landing stage with the bamboo avenue. He also constructed a wall around the Park which however served little purpose; in any case his wife showed little interest in the house or Park. Since all period furniture had been taken away from Barrackpore to the Viceregal establishments, new furniture had to be bought which lacked the elegance of its predecessors. The Second Earl of Lytton tried to revive the fading fortunes by providing new furnishings, *durries* and *shamianas* for use under the banyan tree. Deer were brought

The Lady Hardinge Bridge on the Moti Jheel
© Raj Bhavan Archives, Calcutta

from Barisal in distant East Bengal to create a deer park in a fenced off portion of land near the Cenotaph. Perhaps the Governor remembered his childhood days at Barrackpore, when his father had been the Viceroy and the family spent some time at Barrackpore, dining al fresco under the banyan tree and watching the hawks swoop down.

In 1927 Sir Stanley Jackson built three gatehouses in the north, the east and the west. All three gates were made of wrought iron and bore the Royal Insignia in honour of King George V. Other Governors and their wives messed about the garden, planning a hedge of oleander here or an avenue of frangipani there, building and laying rose gardens and planting carnations, sweet peas and fruit plants as best as they could. Official papers dated 1939 laid out a set of rules for the renewal, maintenance and repair of furnishings at all the official residences of the Government of Bengal in Calcutta, Dacca

The Lotus Fountain at Barrackpore
© Raj Bhavan Archives, Calcutta

The Earl of Ronaldshay

and Darjeeling. The Barrackpore House was included in this list under the Governor's Allowances and Privileges Order of 1937. Sadly enough, a paltry sum of 1908 rupees was allotted for annual maintenance.

For after all what could a cash strapped Governor do in the aftermath of a devastating World War and with a raging Freedom Movement at hand to deal with! Once the capital had moved to Delhi there was little glory for Barrackpore Park thereafter. Built by Wellesley, a solace for Lady Canning, the Park had soared to glory under Lord Curzon. The Minto regime was its swan song. Thereafter it passed through many trials and came to become something of a traveller's halt or a Circuit House in the 1930s. There were the odd moments of fame, like the visit of the Chinese premier Chiang-Kai-Shek and Madam Chiang-Kai-Shek in 1942. On the whole, however, Barrackpore's status had been supplanted by Lutyens' Delhi and the houses at Simla.

In 1943 Barrackpore Park became the centre of government attention again, this time over the lugubrious matter of an American Burial Ground to bury soldiers who had died in World War II in north eastern India and beyond. The Americans, rather poignantly, wanted a site with a number of stipulations: not close to a *bustee*, not open to the depredations of cattle and not part of an existing cemetery. They wanted a piece of land over which the American flag could be allowed to fly. Ultimately, the Americans settled on the land adjoining Lady Canning's tomb and awaited formal permission. Letters flew back and forth between the British and American authorities over the suitability of the request and the provenance of the issue. Questions arose as to whether the Viceroy of India or the Governor of Bengal had legal rights

Aerial Photograph of
Barrackpore Cantonment
during World War II
© National Archives and Records
Administration (NARA)

US Air Tactical Force Headquarters,
Barrackpore, during World War II
© National Archives and Records
Administration (NARA)

opinion on these points.

[signature] 5.5.43   SGE

There might be difficulty in making over any part of the Public Portion of the Park as this was handed over by the Viceroy to the Bengal Government "for the use of the public" - (though even here there is a precedent in the plot at South East corner given by Lord Lytton for erection of a school.)

The Private Portion of Park would be much more directly under His Excellency's personal control and provided the arrangement was in the nature of a permission to the American Army to use a definite area as a burial ground without our resigning ownership of the land there should be no difficulty.

Such area I suggest would be best East of Lady Canning's Tomb which is well concealed from Government House, has a view over the Hooghly to one of the best known and oldest Dutch churches in India, that at Serampore - a view which was selected by Lady Canning as one of the most beautiful in lower Bengal, and also has the advantage that it is already the site of the tomb of the wife of the 1st Governor General of India.

If an area roughly as sketch were enclosed and consecrated by the ecclesiastical Authorities nothing more than a formal permission from His Excellency to the American Army to use it free of any rent for the purpose proposed would appear to be necessary.

There would be free access from the adjoining river side road in the Public Portion of the Park and it would be far quieter than any site near the high road and once consecrated there would be no possibility of subsequent encroachment for any other purpose.

Sketch attached   *R. F. Watson*

S. G. E.
6.5.43.

I mentioned this to P.S.V yesterday. He thought that the Viceroy might have to be consulted, on the ground that the Viceroy continued to exercise some form of control over the Governor in respect of the private portion of the Park at Barrackpore. The Park forms part of one of the "official residences" of the Governor, but this point must be looked up. If S.G.E was no information, would he please refer to M.S.G. If the M.S.G has none, we will see what we have.

[signature] 9.5.43.   SGE

House in Barrackpore

Though the Park is now one of the official residences of the Governor it has only recently become so. SGE

For many years after the Park was made over to Bengal it was only a Circuit House & was maintained as such.

I am sure H.E. the Viceroy did not maintain any personal control after the Park was made over. All Governors Estates were transferred to H.E's portfolio in Sir John Anderson's time so H.E would have to have complete control.

R. F. Watson
9/5/43

Have we any papers in the General of the Special Section?

[signature]
10.5.43

We have no papers either in the General or Special Section on the point raised in Addl. Secretary's note dated the 9-5-43. The Chief Secretary's letter No. 509 P.D. dated the 12-5-36 to the Govt. of India may however be seen. It will be seen that the Govt. House at Barrackpore and the park attached to it were originally the properties of the Govt. of India. The properties were transferred to the Govt. of Bengal in 1921 for use as a Circuit House in exchange for the Belvedere. They were made as an 'Official residence of H.E. the Governor as defined in para. 3 of the Govt. of India (Governors' Allowances and Privileges) Order, 1936 with effect from the 1st April 1937. There is nothing in the discussions in the Political Department file which led to the issue of the Chief Secretary's letter referred to above that H.E. the Viceroy exercised any control over any portion of the park attached to the Barrackpore House under the arrangement made in 1921. If this is correct he cannot perhaps exercise any control under the existing condition. To be sure a reference may be made to the C & W Department who seems to have got the relevant papers of 1921.

P.S.
11.5.43.

Yes.   *[signature]*
Ask for an immediate reply.   11.5.43

12.5.43

Papers relating to the proposed American Cemetery at Barrackpore
© Raj Bhawan Archives, Calcutta

D.O.No. 1029 S

Calcutta,
29th June, 1943.

Dear General,

I am desired to acknowledge, with thanks, your letter of the 24th June, 1943, addressed to His Excellency the Governor, regarding the location of a cemetery site at Barrackpore for use of the United States Army Forces. For the purposes of formal record, I am to say that His Excellency the Governor is pleased to make available, as a cemetery site for the use of the United States Army Forces for such period of time as the need for it shall exist, the following site in the private portion of the Governor Estate at Barrackpore, viz., -

A piece of land measuring 585 ft. on the east side, 280 ft. on the north side and 175 ft on the south side lying in the private portion of the Estate to the north of the river Hooghly to the south of the road leading into the private portion of the Estate, to the east of Government House, Barrackpore, and immediately to the west of the public road running through the public portion of the Estate from the river bank to the entrance to the private portion of the Estate known as the Bamboo Gate. A map of this site is attached herewith.

2. The site is made available without payment of rent, rates or taxes of any kind.

3. The only conditions attaching to its use by the United States Army Forces are -

(1) that there shall not be erected on any part of it any structure which is visible from the main building of Government

---

2

Government House, Barrackpore, itself,
and

(2) that when it is no longer required by the United States Army Forces for use as a cemetery, it shall be formally handed back to the Governor of Bengal for the time being and shall not be used by the United States Army Forces for any other purpose.

4. For the purposes of record and to conclude this transaction, would you kindly let me have in writing a formal acknowledgment of the receipt of this letter and a formal acceptance of the conditions mentioned above.

Yours sincerely,

Addl. Secretary to the Governor.

Brigadier General J. A. Warden,
U. S. Army Commanding.

Papers relating to the proposed American Cemetery at Barrackpore
© Raj Bhawan Archives, Calcutta

Map (hand-drawn) of the proposed American Cemetery at Barrackpore
© Raj Bhawan Archives, Calcutta

over the park and the right to allot the land for the burial ground. Heated tempers led to a clear announcement that the house, having been made part of the Governor of Bengal's Allowance and Privilege Scheme, was no longer a Circuit house but once again part of the Governor's Estate. There were further frayed tempers about the exact site to be given over to the Americans. 'The Eastern Army (without reference to us) have put up some menial quarters and kitchen on part of the site near Lady Canning's tomb. I think they should be advised at once that no buildings should be constructed there,'[5] wrote Captain E.F. White on 25th May 1943.

A month later, a compromise was reached. A site was marked out further north of the one suggested by the Americans. This was done so that the cemetery would be out of view of Government House and would not destroy the canna garden, now disfigured by 'the appallingly ugly structures put up by the Eastern Army.'[6]

The cemetery never materialized but the ugly war sheds are still there, as squat and lumpy as when they were first put up, surrounding Lady Canning's tomb and now used by Police families. In fact, the tin structures were put up by the Americans all over the Park, while the Bengal Governors, shaken by the monstrosities of modern warfare, had little time to put up much of a defence. These 'nissen huts', relics of the War, began the gradual deterioration of the Park's façade.

In 1948 the new government of free India transferred large portions of the Park to the West Bengal Government who used it as a training academy for new recruits to the State Police and as the Brigade Headquarters of the State Armed Police. A portion of the estate around the Flagstaff House was carved out for the use of the Governor of West Bengal. This has today become the Governor's retreat. Years later, the statues of British statesmen that adorned Calcutta's streets found refuge on the lawns of the Flagstaff House.

Government House itself had become a police hospital and was thus shorn of any vestige of romance it might have had. The whirligig of time brought in its revenges, and the ghosts of the Court of Directors, so disapproving of Wellesley's scheme in 1805, might have been soothed by the overgrown grass and weeds that soon took over the rapidly declining mansion.

NOTES ———————————————————————————

1. Private papers from Raj Bhawan Archives, Calcutta.
2. Ibid.
3. Bence-Jones, Mark. 1982. The Viceroys of India. Constable.
4. Pal, A.C. 1931. The Park at Barrackpore AD 1785- 1931. Private Secretary's Press.
5. Private papers from Raj Bhawan Archives, Calcutta.
6. Ibid.

CHAPTER FOURTEEN

THE GARDEN OF DELIGHT

❝

"It was in a sorry state when I visited Barrackpore in 1967, and the garden had a neglected and melancholy air; the park could hardly be seen for new and unsightly buildings."

Palaces of the Raj
Magnificence and Misery of the Lord Sahibs
Mark Bence-Jones

❞

As the British expanded their territories in India they built a series of structures related to administration, education, health, recreation as well as private residences. Barrackpore Park contains all these. The Governor General's mansion was surrounded by a menagerie, a church, a school and a cemetery, everything in fact except for a hospital. There were also a couple of bungalows built into the Park from its earliest days. Government House, Barrackpore began as a majestic idea to complement the even grander palace of British India's Government House, Calcutta. Ultimately, however, the palace morphed into a large country mansion with an eight columned portico on its northern façade, now lost.

The bungalow was the greatest legacy of colonial rule. The term itself was adopted from the word *bangla*, a tribute to the original Bengali modules on which they were built and in early Company records they were variously spelt as '*bangalo*' or '*bungaloo*'.

In the first part of the 17th century the bungalow implied a *kutcha* house made of mud brick and a rush-thatched roof. As time passed this evolved into an oblong structure with a pyramidal roof, either with mud tiles or ornate wooden castellations. The verandah was extended by a portico with potted plants and a lordly entry was achieved by growing trellised creepers. The verandahs were embellished

Bungalow number 1, Barrackpore Park, 2019
© Abhijit Sarkar

with typical colonial furniture including rugs, rattan chairs, potted plants and the planter's chair.

Many of these ivy covered cottages were part of the British impulse of creating pockets of Englishness. The imperial hill-stations which the British established to recover from the heat of the plains had bungalows and cottages with poetic names like Tinker Bell's Cottage, Catherine Villa, The Eyrie and even Yarrows. The British established almost ninety hill-stations including Matheran near Bombay, Ooty near Madras, Nainital and Mussoorie near Dehradun, Darjeeling near Calcutta and the grandest of all Simla – the summer capital near New Delhi.

Alongside the bungalows richer people as well as administrators lived in mansions which were large, impressive square buildings with flat roofs, porticoes, venetian blinds, tall pillars and immense gates. These neo-classical mansions were the pride of Calcutta, Bombay and Madras. In the 20th century when Edwin Lutyens was tasked with the project of creating India's new capital at New Delhi, he chose Barrackpore's bungalows, especially the Flagstaff House as a model for the new bungalows.

When the cantonment had first been built, some pre-existing bungalows, as has already been noted, had been absorbed into the premises. The first pictorial representations of Barrackpore show these

Honeymoon Lodge, Barrackpore Park
Unknown Photographer
© The British Library Board

thatched bungalows. In Wellesley's time the bungalows grouped around the main house were thatched cottages while Lord Minto describes them as being of a 'swiss style'. For Emily Eden the bungalows were extremely convenient as the visitors could be worn out by all the travelling to and fro, thus being of no trouble at all. 'They come to breakfast and go back immediately to their bungalows utterly exhausted, poor things!'[1]

During the time of Viceroy Elgin, in 1864, the roofs of bungalows number 1 and 2 were pulled down and replaced by terraced roofs. To the north west of the Government House was a bungalow known as the Flagstaff House. It was named after

the flagstaff of Admiral Watson's ship, the HMS Kent, which had been damaged in a battle with the French in 1757 and was placed on the lawn bordering the riverbank. The original Flagstaff House was built in 1828 and had a thatched roof; when the roof burned down it was known as the 'pora kutir' in Bengali which literally meant 'the burnt cottage'.

The Honeymoon Lodge or bungalow number 3 derived its name from the fact that it was frequently lent to newly-weds who arrived in Barrackpore as the Governor General's guest. It was yet another popular cottage having all the characteristics of a classical bungalow. Distinguished guests who stayed

Photo. Bourne & Shephera

MYALL KING'S GRAVE

William Beresford at Myall King's Grave
© Bourne & Shepherd

here for their wedding trip included Hannah More, Lord Macaulay's sister and her husband Sir Charles Trevelyan, the well known British civil servant. This bungalow was later officially made the residence of the Military Secretary to the Viceroy. The most well known military secretary was Sir William Beresford, who served three Viceroys – Ripon, Dufferin and Landsdowne. Beresford's horse Myall King was buried close to the bungalow. Myall King was a prize horse who had won a series of races in Calcutta including the Calcutta Viceroy's Cup, the Lucknow Steward's Purse and the Hyderabad Gold Cup between 1887 and 1892.

The Bandmaster's Bungalow had been built on the bank of the Moti Jheel by Sir John Lawrence. The Bandmaster found no use for it, though, and the house accommodated the ayahs who accompanied visitors.

The Railway Station at Barrackpore, 1867
© Trustees of the Victoria Memorial Hall, Calcutta

The Park Superintendent's House was built in 1823 in the public portion of the Park, close to the river. The Stable Superintendent's Bungalow was also built in the Park, near the east gate, in 1864 and was popularly known as the Coachman's Bungalow.

The Eden School, now renamed as the Barrackpore Park Government School, still stands in the south-east end of the park, near the main road. There was also a Masonic Lodge, established in 1870. A new Lodge called the Ubique Lodge No 2467 was built in 1893 and used as a Club House for the golfers. It is at present a popular hotel.

The Garrison Church was used by both the military officers as well as the Governor General. Hariot Dufferin remembers it by its huge swinging *punkahs* that almost blew the church down, while Emily Eden dismissed it waspishly as 'a very full church; not a good sermon' and 'there are seven regiments

Garrison Church now called St Bartholomew's Cathedral, 2017
© Abhijit Sarkar

quartered here, so our congregation was very red and clanking.'[2]

Once upon a time Barrackpore Park was an important getaway for the British in Bengal. All who came to Calcutta and were important enough to merit the Governor General or Viceroy's attention came also to Barrackpore. The list of visitors who journeyed up the official barge *Soonamookie* or *The Maud* and later *Queen Mary* reads like a composite picture of the British-Indian world. They included royalty and nobility, like the Prince of Wales, later King George V and his consort Queen Mary (1906),

the next Prince of Wales (1921), the Crown Prince Wilhelm of Germany (1911), the Crown Prince of Sweden (1924) and the King and Queen of Belgium (1925). Newly-exiled Eastern potentates were sent to Barrackpore for safekeeping, as in the case of the exiled Amir of Afghanistan Dost Muhammad, or the young Maharajah Duleep Singh.

Other distinguished men who were important in the task of administration were treated in style by the Viceroy at Barrackpore. Winston Churchill spent time here, as did Sir Stamford Raffles. Bishop Heber had his first ever elephant-ride at the Park and

Plantains at Barrackpore
Edward Lear
© Harvard University, Houghton Library

A scatter of artists, both amateur and professional, came to Barrackpore and were followed by photographers who had begun working in India from the 1860s onwards. Most of the painters who worked upon scenes of Barrackpore life were foreigners, with the exception of Sita Ram. Perhaps there were others, still to be in the public domain. Like sculpture, painting and drawing relies on the artists' personal imagination and perception. The paintings of Barrackpore that have survived and fill the pages of this book convey what the outsider wanted to highlight - that India was a land of riotous colour and spectacle. At other places artists arranged the landscape to heighten the sense of the picturesque and created a carefully wrought and crafted representation, in which ruins, temples, mosques, servants, tribesmen, mountains, rivers as well as fascinating props like the *hookah*, drapes and jewellery were painted.

In Barrackpore, artists usually sketched the garden and its vegetation, the unfamiliar flowers and trees, the animals in the menagerie and the river that flowed past. Many of the painters were botanists like Nathaniel Wallich or Francis Buchanan who sought to reproduce the natural history of unfamiliar species. Others were the First Ladies like Emily Eden and Charlotte Canning who drew bird and plume to send home for English eyes who had never been to India.

A few artists came out to India with commissions to paint spectacular Indian scenery. One such was Edward Lear who visited India during the time of Lord Northbrooke. Lear had been invited by the Viceroy himself, who stood all expenses of the visit. The sketch of the banyan tree of Barrackpore Park that has been used for this book's cover was made in December 1873 during a three-week stay in

marvelled at the strange animals of the menagerie as he was shown around by Lord Amherst. William Carey crossed the river from yonder Serampore to parley with the First Lord Minto.

Dashing soldiers, pious priests, noblemen like the British peer Lord Valentia and numbers of women travellers including Fanny Parks, Emma Roberts and Maria Graham gaped at the animals, commented approvingly on the tranquil green parkland and stopped to sketch, paint and re-make the beauty of Barrackpore through brush and colour.

Golf Club now Ubique Hotel,
Barrackpore, 2019
© Abhijit Sarkar

Ruins of Plant &
Seed House, 2017
© Amitabha Karkun

Bungalow in ruins, Barrackpore,
2018
© Abhijit Sarkar

More moments of leisure
© The Trustees of the
Bowood Collection

Calcutta. Though it seems to be a rough sketch rather than a finished one, the colours and strokes capture the depth of the tree, its roots, the river flowing beyond and the one solitary gardener standing on the bare brown earth almost merging with the colours. In Lear's words, 'Drew off and on till 4 - when given some cold turkey and beer; very acceptable. Walk on terraces and to Lady Canning's tomb; the light and climate are like those of a fine sultry summer evening in England. Poinciana Regia foliage particularly rich and lovely.'[3]

The garden was always the delight of all the residents of Government House. Some, like Emily Eden and Charlotte Canning spent happy hours gardening, while others, though not actively participating in the creation of neatly trimmed lawns and gloriously blooming beds, enjoyed the flowers much the same. To go through all the memoirs, journals, letters and reminiscences of Barrackpore is to see a riot of flowers like bougainvillea, pink lotus, blue convolvulus, plumeria, poinsettia, climbing roses, carnations, marigolds, honeysuckle and poppy, amaryllis and oleander. The palms and mango trees and bamboo grew alongside the camellia, mignonette and ivy, the cowslips and snowdrops, the peonies and roses.

But the pride of the garden was the Great Banyan tree. Standing to the south of the Goverment House, it was said to be around two hundred and forty years old in 1925. The tree had been there before the East India Company bought land in Barrackpore. The parent trunk may have been destroyed in the cyclone of 1864 but it had about four hundred arterial roots spreading out. From the time of Charlotte Canning it was used as a sit-out, its branches forming a canopy over the guests as the squirrels chattered and the mynas sang and the jackals slunk in and out.

The tree stands proud and tall till today, framing the house in much the same way as Charlotte Canning had painted in 1858. In a world that has grown weary and old and stale, perhaps it stands outside time.

❦

NOTES

1.	Eden, Emily and Eden, Fanny. 1872. Letters from India. Richard Bentley and Son. Edited by Eleanor Eden.
2.	Ibid.
3.	Dehejia, Vidya. 1990. Impossible Picturesqueness: Edward Lear's Indian Watercolours, 1873-1875. With an essay by Allen Staley. Columbia University Press.

CHAPTER FIFTEEN

AN OVERVIEW

> "*It is in a crumbling, dilapidated state...this should be declared as a heritage building.*"

Letter written in 2012 to the Governor of West Bengal
Amitabha Karkun

Barrackpore Park was constructed as a new seat of relaxation for the Governor General but from the very beginning it was a fascinating point of contestation between British culture and Indian identity. It was built to mark the turn of the East India Company's fortunes, from a mercantile body to a governing identity with wide, often wrongly used powers. The house and park was a visual reminder of British authority and superiority. Its gardens and parkland were deliberately English in design and layout. The estate was also out of bounds for Indians and was treated as an inviolable private space, a sacred white-only zone which represented a sanctuary, where one might retreat and be cleansed before meeting the rigours of duty and administration that Calcutta represented. Here the Governor General and his family could ride, play

chess, write letters, complete journals, sketch, hunt, have private meals with only the closest acquaintances and recover from the enervating climate. The heat of India was a constant point of reference for British administrators and they spent much of their time ferreting out spaces for convalescence and rest. Simla, Mussoorie, Darjeeling, Coonoor, Ooty would come later. Barrackpore was the oldest retreat.

Along with gardening, the estate also provided a place for British culture. Its facilities like a greenhouse, an aviary, a menagerie, were part of the grand British ideal of the healthy outdoor. One could dine under the banyan tree in a tribute to that very British activity of tea in the garden, though the kites, hawks and parakeets had to be

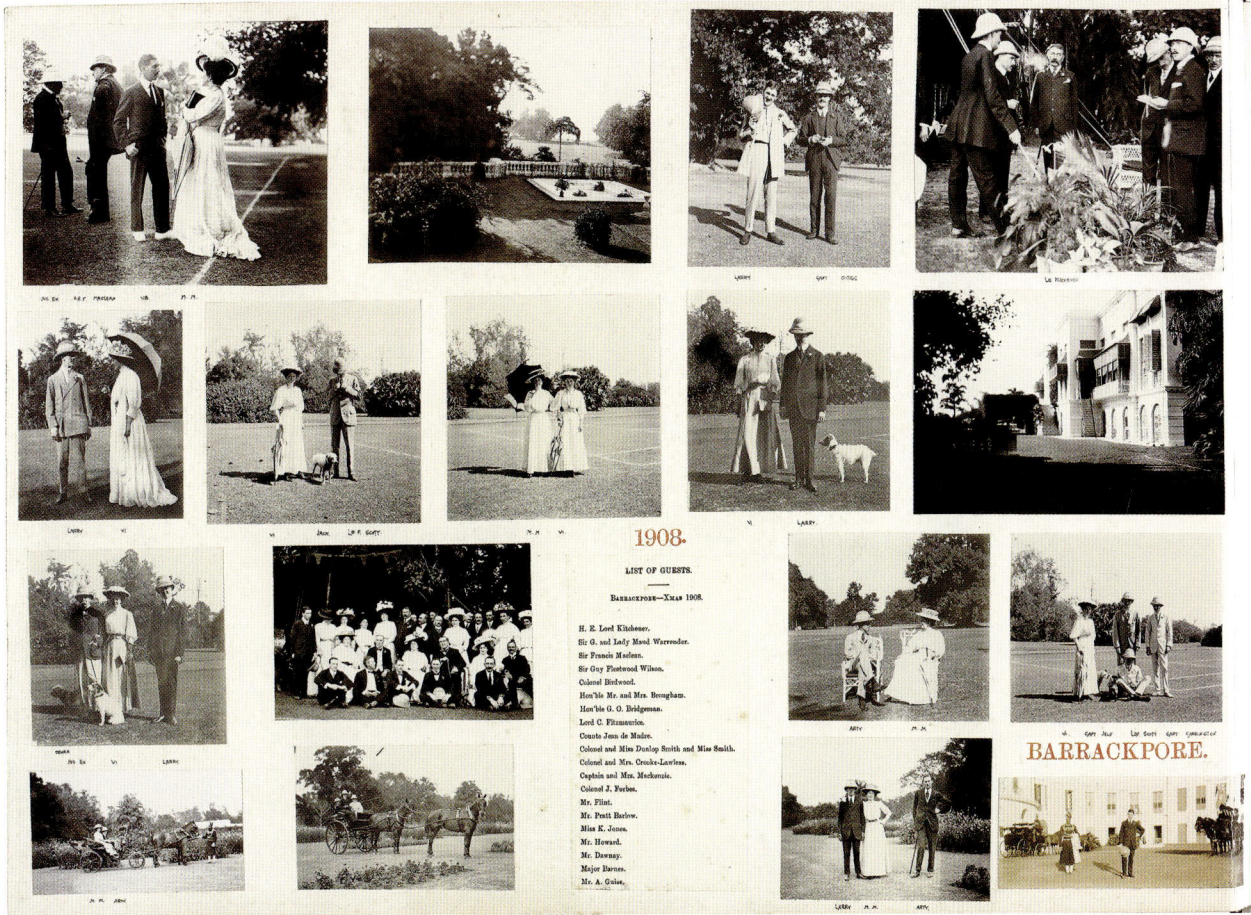

Christmas at Barrackpore Park, 1908
© Timothy Melgund, 7th Earl of Minto

imaginatively transformed into finches and thrushes carolling on a spring day in an English garden. There was no need to wait for the sun to come out from behind the dark English clouds. The sun beat down on them all the time in tropical vengeance, but as long as the muslin gowns and bonnets could provide shade, one could always pretend that it was an approximation of home.

In later years Vicereines would play croquet, practice golf and go to the races. The Barrackpore Church and the burial ground completed this re-creation of an English country house. One would have expected a scattering of graves of beloved pets where the faithful Chance or Dandy and Fluff were buried; but either the graves have been lost, or, as in the latter half of the 19th century the animals accompanied the Lord Sahib to Simla and were interred there. William Beresford's prize horse, Myall King, was however buried here and an obelisk in his name, with its poetic inscription, endures till today.

Government House Barrackpore, 2018
View from the top during restoration
© Nikhil Kapur

Many wives of the Governor General fancied themselves to be amateur botanists and spent hours at Barrackpore sketching plants and flowers, growing fancy shrubs and using their stay in India to acquaint themselves with newly discovered specimens. Lady Amherst and Emily Eden took regular walks with the Director of the Botanic Gardens, Nathaniel Wallich, to gain useful botanical knowledge. Lord Auckland tried to grow strawberries here and possibly Barrackpore is the first place in India where this very English fruit made its appearance.

Sometimes Empire imprinted itself on England's national consciousness. The exotic appeal of India often turned into a fetish for collecting markers of colonial rule and sending them home. Animals and birds were shipped to Britain as specimens of what overseas rule had achieved and were used to define the mysterious East. Lady Amherst shipped home an ornamental pheasant bred in Barrackpore Park, though native to Burma, and introduced it to her home in Bedfordshire in 1828. In time the bird came to be known as Lady Amherst's Pheasant and specimens survived till 2015. Charles Trevelyan, a civil servant and later Governor of Madras, sent home a male rhinoceros from the Barrackpore menagerie in 1864 which died a heartrending death the following year from improper feeding. Lord Mayo sent home an elephant in 1868 which died in transit.

Ruins of the menagerie, 2010

Lady Mayo kept a tiger cub as a pet at Calcutta which followed her around tamely till it grew too big and fierce, whereupon it was sent to Barrackpore. Anglo Indian officers shipped home to England a range of animals including leopards, monkeys and parrots. Lord Hardinge presented a tiger to Queen Victoria. One can only wonder at the grim suffering the animals must have endured on their voyage out and in the unfamiliar environs of a Northern climate.

Most of the memsahibs at Barrackpore maintained albums or commonplace books which contained pressed flowers, leaves, insects as well as sketches of the strange land and the people they encountered. Emily Eden sketched everything, from princes and potentates to birds, flowers, ghats, gardeners, children, temples and a hundred other ephemera. Charlotte Canning used watercolours to create albums of visual splendour, in which the Indian landscape was rendered in a thousand lights and colours, an exercise that exorcised the raging violence of the Mutiny by reducing India to a series of picturesque views. The colonial master could turn the turbulence of the seething land into the ordered symmetry of the painting, while retaining the gaze of the colonial master, surveying everything from a distance, serene and balanced.

Lucki Petcha Bengal
Painted at Barrackpore under the supervision of
John Fleming (1747-1829)

The Great Exhibition: India No. 1, 1851
The ivory and jewel encrusted thrown presented to Queen Victoria
by The Maharaja of Travancore
Joseph Nash
© Royal Collection Trust

The Great Exhibition: India No. 2, 1851
Some of the exhibits including saddle trappings and arms
Joseph Nash
© Royal Collection Trust

British attitudes towards Indians, indeed all non-English cultures were usually one of scorn. The paintings and photographs of Barrackpore Park that are extant show a scattering of Indians in clearly menial positions, caddies, gardeners, *khidmatgars* or syces, grooms and guards, boatmen or *ayahs* and other such. Emily Eden had her Rosina and Mary Curzon had Ramdass, but to most other ladyships the servants were a vast but anonymous congregation. The Marquess of Hastings had the Indian Sita Ram paint so many watercolours to complement his journal but never mentions him by name in his writings; in one place he speaks of 'a Bengal draftsman' who accompanied him in his travels but nothing more.

Once photography came to India, photographs provided a visual complement to political craft. In one of the earliest photographs of Barrackpore taken of Lady Canning, the future Vicereine is shown to be comforting English women who had survived the horrors of the Mutiny. The set of seven photographs that Samuel Bourne took in 1867 show Government House and its grounds as an ordered, peaceful place, serving a visual picture of a site that had recently been associated with traumatic British experiences. The Barrackpore set of photographs was released at a fitting time and was commercially successful. The Mutiny of 1857 had originated here before spreading to the rest of India. Bourne's photographs are an act of assurance, showing a placid land, with Indian servants grouped humbly around the parkland and no hint of the horrors and violence that was the present day actuality. The Viceroy's house and garden was as neat and systematic as ever, the rebels were properly subdued and the park and house were safely visitable.

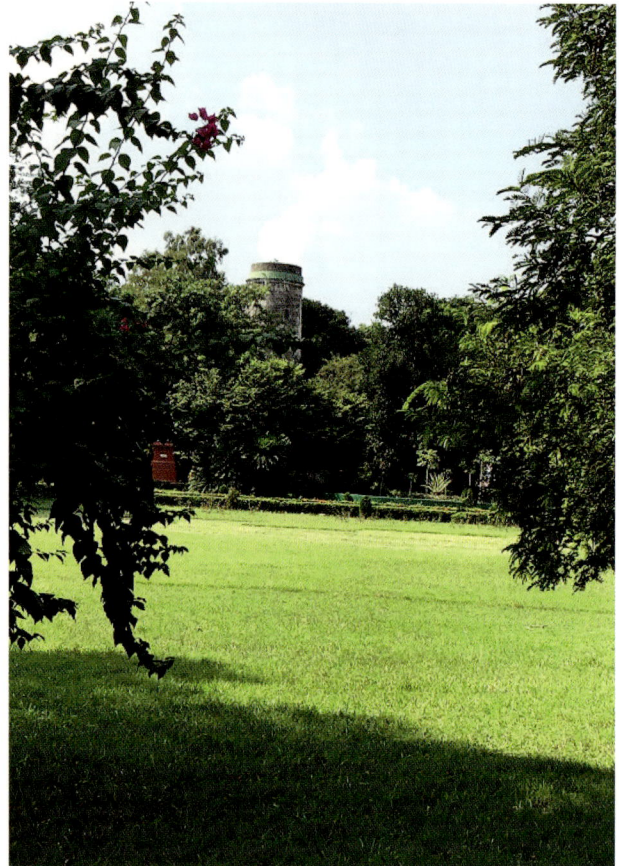

Semaphore on the lawns of Flagstaff House, 2018
© Monabi Mitra

Military Cemetery, Barrackpore, 2018
© Abhijit Sarkar

Statues on the grounds
of Flagstaff House, 2018
© Abhijit Sarkar

Imperialism was sustained in India by so many diverse ways: collaboration with the languid and loyal Princely states, force over the more ambitious and resistant ones and a deliberate typecasting of the rest of India as untrustworthy and benighted.

Ultimately Barrackpore was always synonymous with the fragility of Indo-British relations. From the first Revolt of 1824, the Bengal army had proved to be filled with dissidents. The Bengal army had initially comprised upper class recruits from Oudh and Bihar who were predominantly Brahmins or Rajputs. Their caste identity determined their living habits and most sepoys lived in their own huts, cooked their own meals and grouped around their own clans. Once the sepoys turned mutinous in 1824 the British realized that caste based kinship had to be displaced by racial constructs of superiority; in time this hardened into racial assumptions of the hardy Pathan, the fierce Sikhs, the effete Bengali, the skilled Mussalman and the devious Hindu.

Over time sepoys began to be distrusted and the events of 1857 resulted in extreme exaggerations of racial threat. Significantly, both the revolts of 1824 and 1857 had occurred at Barrackpore which assumed a symbolic value for the British. The revolts had occurred in the cantonment adjoining the Governor General's house, thereby emphasizing both the impudence of the attacks as well as the vulnerability of the British. It is no coincidence that the British withdrew to Simla after 1857 and to Delhi after 1911. Barrackpore and later Calcutta was too potent a reminder of the counter attacking Indians. In Delhi, the Mughals had been long decimated to pass out of popular memory and there was a feeling that one could start all over again. Self identities are complex things; they cause a confused medley of emotions. Just as the British created their own private spaces in Barrackpore Park, Calcutta and Simla, so too did Indians demand new icons after independence. The Cawnpore Memorial, with its Angel of the Resurrection statue designed by Charlotte Canning was an iconic reminder of the massacre of women and children at the Bibighar during the Mutiny; in 1947 it was partly defaced by Indians before being reinstated in a church. Its place was taken by a statue of Tantia Tope, one of the generals of the Rani of Jhansi, as a celebration of the Indian cause. Similarly, statues of British statesmen, military commanders and monarchs were removed from public places throughout India.

In Calcutta the substitution was the largest as scores of British statues were taken off Calcutta's thoroughfares and distributed to the Flagstaff House, the country retreat in Barrackpore of the Governer of West Bengal. Others were sent to the Victoria Memorial Hall, Calcutta. The present writers had attempted in the year 2005 to bring those placed in the Flagstaff House to a Park near the Victoria Memorial Hall, to allow a new generation of millennials to come to terms with the historical event of colonial rule. Many of the sculptures were important landmarks in the history of statuary, like the ones made by C. H. Foley, and were appreciated by art historians worldwide for their dexterous artistry; it was hoped that they would be displayed in this spirit rather than being seen as disturbing reminders of a difficult past. The then Governor, a member of the Gandhi family, surprisingly declined the request. In an article about the statues of Flagstaff House, published by Raj Bhavan later, the same Governor described them with considerable zeal; perhaps his refusal to part with them for a more public preening was less about nationalistic concerns and more to do with real affection for the silent spectators in his garden.

In a twist of fate, one of the co-authors of this book has been posted to the West Bengal Police Training Branch for the last three years and has the care of Government House, Barrackpore today. Stumbling about amongst the overgrown park, now unrecognizable from what it was a hundred years ago, he rediscovered the building. Efforts are on to restore it and bring some vestige of its former glory back again.

The time has come to revisit Barrackpore Park as a legitimate part of India's past. If the pages of history have come alive above, at least a part of that quest has been fulfilled.

Aviary Pond with restored Nissen Hut at night, 2019
© Abhijit Sarkar

CHAPTER SIXTEEN
RUIN AND RENEWAL

“

"The marble fountain from Agra is cracked and
ruinous, the house dilapidated and the grounds given
over to the police. But it's all still there..."

Splendours of the Raj
Philip Davis

”

Barrackpore Park and Government House, Barrackpore was the culmination of growing British power as its Empire rose in new and unfamiliar lands. Bit by bit Lord sahibs and Lady sahibs created a weekend retreat that reminded them of the manor houses and gardens left behind at home.

Remains of the northern façade of Government House without the Tuscan columned portico, 2017

Rebuilding of the Tuscan columned portico on the northern facade of Government House, 2019

155 | Under the Banyan Tree

North western façade of Government House, 2012

North eastern façade of Government House, 2012

With the end of the Raj the house and park began to accommodate new India's needs and as administrative buildings sprang up to house the Police training academy, the older structures fell into disuse. Barrackpore itself became derided as a remnant of an outmoded colonial order and while the Cantonment functioned as a military area, the Governor General's house became derelict.

In 2015 a half-hearted effort was begun to rescue the building and parkland from oblivion but it took three years for the project to make an energetic start. By then there was an understanding amongst preservationists that rather than being seen as reminders of a merciless colonial bondage, the grounds and buildings had heritage value as representatives of a certain time in India's historical past. Government House was enlisted in the list of the West Bengal Heritage Commission as a heritage building of great significance.

Western façade of Government House, 2012
The varandah block has collapsed but plans are on to reconstruct it.

Western facade of Government House after initial restoration, 2018.
The columned verandah will be rebuilt soon.

This photo-essay traces the journey of Barrackpore Park from near ruination and certain destruction to a heritage zone that exists as an example of a hybrid British-Indian architectural past. By doing so it is hoped that the gardens and buildings are seen as art objects as well as embodying social meanings that include questions of space, identity and cultural politics.

Government House

Various facades of Government House, Barrackpore before restoration, including views from the south, east and the north are presented here. The interiors were in an advanced state of disrepair while the hospital beds and tables belong to a time when police personnel were sent here for recovery.

Eastern façade of Government House, 2012

Eastern façade of Government House during restoration, 2018

Eastern facade of Government House during restoration, 2019

Eastern facade of Government House during restoration, 2019

Southern façade of Government House, before restoration, 2012

Southern façade of Government House, before restoration, 2014

Southern façade of Government House, during restoration, 2017

Southern façade of Government House, during restoration, 2018

Southern façade of Government House, during restoration, 2018

Southern façade of Government House, after restoration, 2019

First floor of Government House during restoration, 2018

Caved-in roof of the first floor of
Government House before restoration, 2015

Caved-in roof of the first floor of Government House, 2015

The oculus on the ceiling of the first floor of Government
House before restoration, 2015

Western portion of the ground floor of Government House
before restoration, 2015

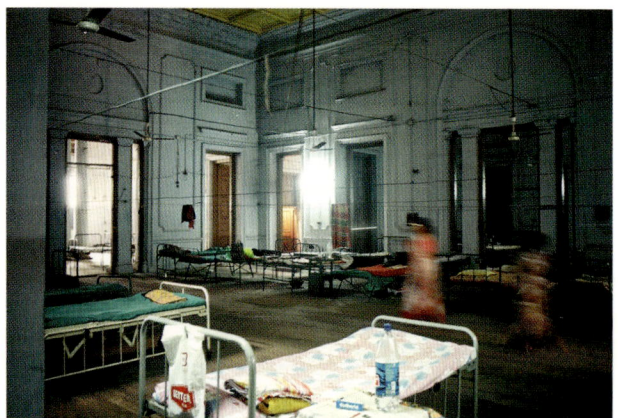
Sprung dance floor of Government House used as a hospital
ward before restoration, 2015

Westside Gallery

The ground floor of the Government House was used to accommodate the servants of the Governors General. At present the restored portion of the ground floor is called the Westside Gallery. Apart from the Memorabilia store and the Lounge, it houses *Wellesley* - a gallery on the history of Barrackpore Park, *Buchanan* - an audio-visual interaction room and *The Arms Gallery* displaying old weapons seized by the Police before 1947. The Westside Gallery was set up in 2019. The other rooms which are now being restored on the ground floor are planned to be used for other temporary and permanent theme-based galleries and exhibitions.

Wellesley - a gallery on the history of Barrackpore Park, 2019

Buchanan - an audio-visual interaction room, 2019

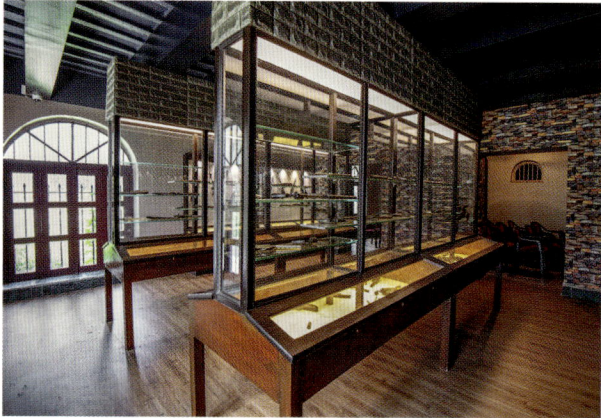

The Arms Room, 2019

The Lounge, 2019

The Memorabilia Store, 2019

Bungalow # 2

Bungalow # 2 is amongst the three oldest bungalows that still remain in Barrackpore Park, the others being Bungalow #1 and Honeymoon Lodge or Bungalow #3. All the three bungalows were re-built in 1864 in the time of Lord Elgin by removing thatched roof bungalows that previously existed there. It is said that these three bungalows provided the architectural model for similar bungalows built subsequently all over British India. This particular bungalow has been repaired and is now being used as a sick bay for the trainees of the State Police Academy.

Bungalow #2 before restoration, 2016

Bungalow # 2 before restoration, 2016

Bungalow # 2 after restoration, 2018

The Gates

The four Gates and Gatehouses which surround Barrackpore Park were built by Lord Wellesley in the early 19th century. While the south gate continues to remain the same the other three were rebuilt in 1927 by Sir Stanley Jackson, Governor of Bengal.

The West Gate connects Barrackpore Park to the Cantonment. It is fronted by St Bartholomew's Cathedral, built in 1831 and used as the Garrison Church for the Cantonment as well as by the Governor General.

The West Gate was in a shabby state of disrepair with a crumbling gatehouse before its restoration in 2018.

Gatehouse of West Gate before restoration, 2016

West Gate before restoration, 2016

Gatehouse of West Gate after restoration, 2017

West Gate after restoration, 2018

The South Gate almost 200 years old today, was the entrance from the Barrackpore Trunk Road that connected Calcutta to Barrackpore.

The North Gate opens out onto the Station Road which connects the Cantonment with the railway station. Adjacent to the North Gate is the Aviary Pond, the remains of the old aviary and the old Golf Link which no longer exists.

Gatehouse of South Gate before restoration, 2017

Gatehouse of South Gate during restoration, 2018

Gatehouse of the South Gate during restoration, 2018

Gatehouse of South Gate during restoration, 2019

Gatehouse of South Gate after restoration, 2019

Gatehouse of North Gate before restoration, 2017

Gatehouse of North Gate after restoration, 2018

Minto Fountain

The Minto Fountain had been designed and constructed in the time of Lord Minto in the early years of the 20th century. Originally a large stone basin with a fountain, 40 feet in diameter and holding 23,000 gallons of water, it was intended to be at the centre of the Curzon-Minto Rose Garden. With engineering difficulties the fountain was placed east of the Aviary Pond in the Minto Garden. It was often used as a swimming pool by succeeding Governors of Bengal. Today the garden has disappeared in a maze of houses and buildings but the fountain somehow remains and was restored along with the rest of the park in 2018.

Minto Fountain before restoration, 2016

Minto Fountain after restoration, 2017

The Lotus Fountain

The Lotus Fountain of Emperor Shah Jahan's vintage had been brought by the Marquess of Hastings in 1815 from Agra Fort and placed on the southern garden of the Government House. It miraculously survived desecration for two hundred years before being made functional again in 2017.

Lotus Fountain before restoration, 2012

Lotus Fountain before restoration, 2014

Lotus Fountain during restoration, 2016

Lotus Fountain after restoration, 2018

Lakes

Moti Jheel, Aviary Pond, Serpentine Lake, Horse-shoe Lake

Barrackpore Park is dotted with lakes which were dug up at different times. The Moti Jheel, the Aviary Pond, the Serpentine Lake as well as the Horse-shoe Lake have, over the centuries, shrunk under weeds and hyacinth. They were dredged and the banks cleared as part of the restoration project. The Lady Hardinge Bridge over the Moti Jheel was repaired and the Lake's connectivity with the river

Lady Hardinge Bridge on the Moti Jheel before restoration, 2012

Moti Jheel after dredging, 2017

Lady Hardinge Bridge on Moti Jheel after restoration, 2017

Hooghly has been restored. Two single-jet fountains have also been installed on either side of the Lady Hardinge Bridge.

The Aviary Pond takes its name from its proximity to the Aviary which had been built by Lord Amherst. A single-jet fountain has been installed and a Nissen Hut, erected during World War II on its bank, has been renovated to make a Lounge commemorating the War.

Serpentine Lake, 2019

The Serpentine and the Horse-shoe lakes have been cleaned but the trees and dense undergrowth surrounding them have not been disturbed so as to serve as a shelter for the wildlife of the park.

Serpentine Lake, 2019

Horse-shoe Lake, 2019

Aviary Pond, 2016

Aviary Pond, 2018

Restored Nissen Hut converted into the World War II Lounge adjacent to Aviary Pond, 2019

The Aviary and other ruins

The Aviary had passed out of public memory from the time the grounds were declared a protected area. During the renovation of Barrackpore Park in 2018, remains of the old Aviary were fortuitously discovered behind a mass of weeds, creepers and jungle on the northern side of the Aviary pond. Ruins of the Park Superintendent's Bungalow as also the Governor General's Dairy have also been located near the Serpentine Lake.

Ruins of the Aviary, 2018

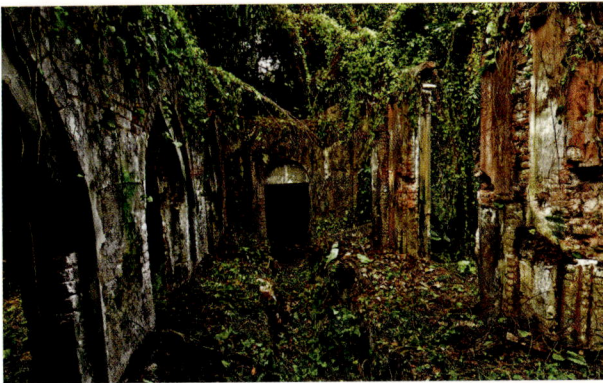

Ruins of the Aviary, 2018

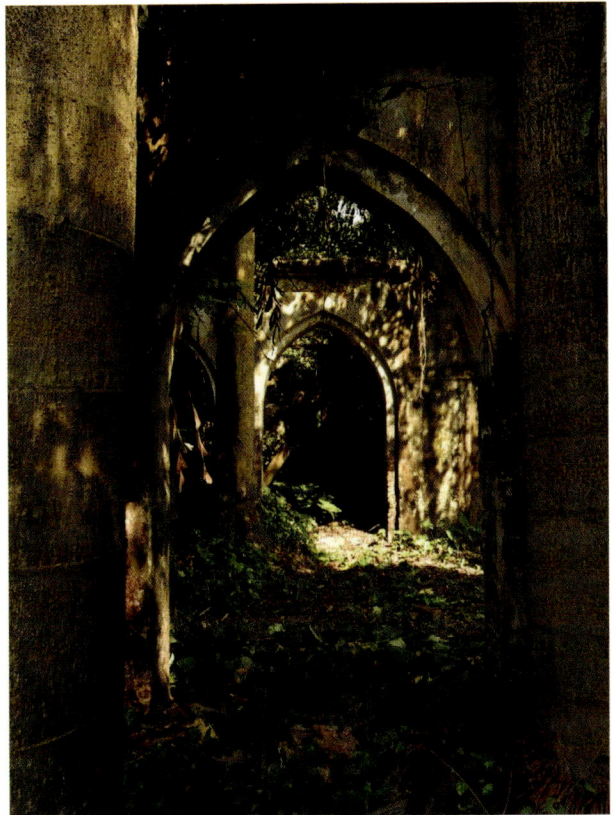

Ruins of the Aviary, 2018

Park Superintendent's Bungalow in ruins, 2019

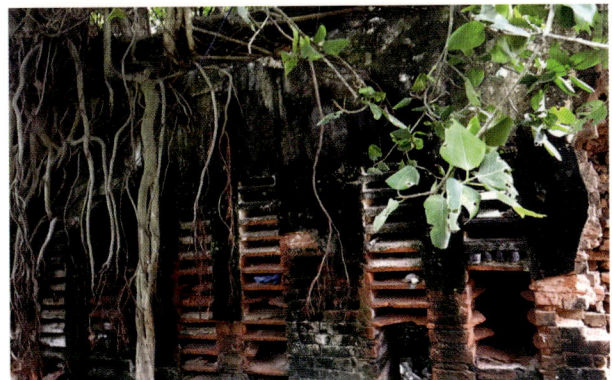

Governor General's Dairy in ruins, 2019

Flagstaff House

The Flagstaff House was built in 1828 for the Private Secretary to the Governor General. The verandahs were later added by Lord Auckland in 1836. Originally a thatched bungalow, it was burnt down and replaced by a terraced roof. Since 1947 the bungalow has been used as a country retreat by the Governor of West Bengal. In 1969, colonial era statues removed from the streets of Calcutta were placed on the grounds of the bungalow adjoining the Cenotaph and the Semaphore.

Flagstaff House, 2019

Cannings' Corner

Lady Canning was buried south of the Government House in 1861. In the late 1960s when statuary of British administrators was removed from the cities to erase memories of the Raj, some statues were placed on the grounds of the Flagstaff House. Lord Canning's statue was placed at a spot in front of his wife's tomb.

The circular iron railing that surrounded the tomb was lost over time. In 2018 the original stones demarcating the enclosure were retrieved from other areas of the park and put up again while attempts are on to reconstruct the cast iron railing with its intricate lettering.

Lady Canning's tomb and Lord Canning's statue before restoration, 2014

Lady Canning's tomb and Lord Canning's statue, 2018

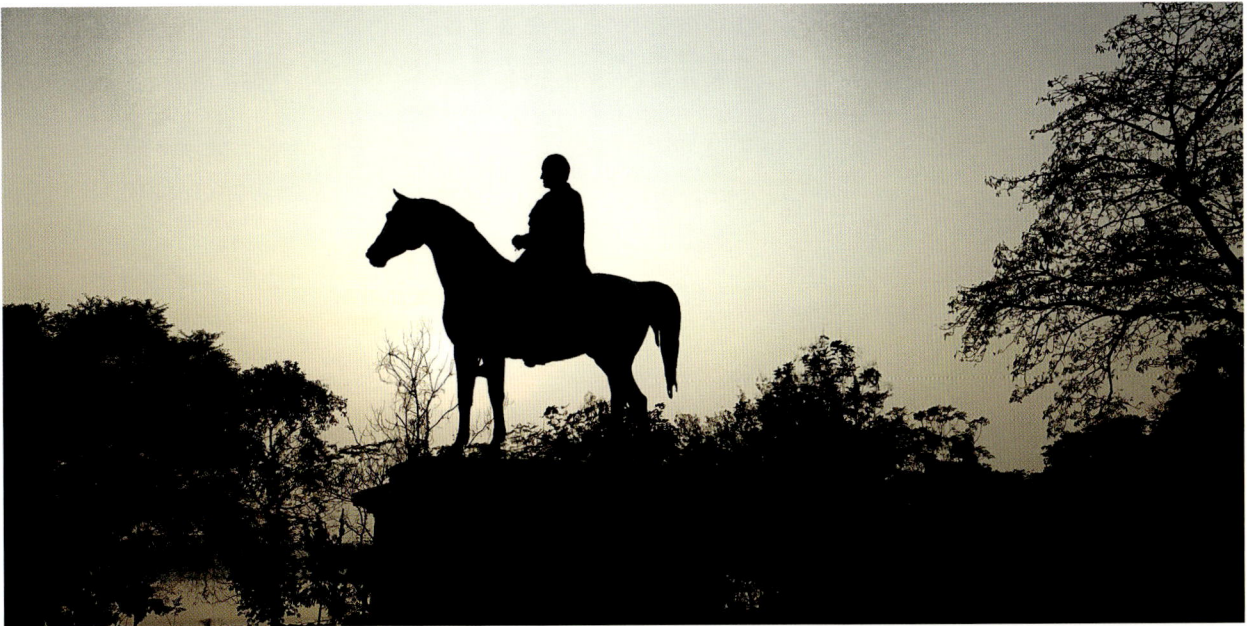

Statue of Lord Canning, 2019

EPILOGUE

At Government House, Barrackpore it is evening and the year is 2019. There is feverish activity all around. Swinging on the scaffolding on the walls are a group of workmen in jeans and sweat-shirts, putting the final splashes of paint on the newly washed and plastered building. The sundial put in by Lord Elgin is lost forever, but a reconstruction has been placed in its original spot. The Lotus Fountain of Shah Jahan's vintage has been cleaned and is spurting merry jets of water. The lawns are being re-dug, flowers are beginning to bloom in beds, the gatehouses have been rescued, cemented and painted. The Moti Jheel has been dredged, Lady Hardinge's bridge repaired and the Honeymoon Lodge has been done up and is being lived in once again. Near the banyan tree the hawks and parakeets still swoop about and jackals slink around the bushes and trot away quickly.

A hundred and fifty years later there is hope that all is not lost and the house can be put back on track again. As a valuable relic of India's past, it is now recognized as a heritage house and attempts are on to restore it as such. Beyond the pathway, down which the Cannings and Elgins and Curzons walked, lies the river, once described in 1813 as one of the busiest and most beautiful scenes ever 'On one side the picturesque boats of the natives, with their floating huts; on the other the bolios and pleasure boats of the English, with their sides of green and gold, and silken streamers.'[1]

As Government House, Barrackpore struggles to raise itself up again, the river lies slumbering and peaceful in the twilight of a 21st century evening. Perhaps a home-grown Griffin will sail past it someday in the future and raise a toast to the house and its bygone glory:

> ' Here from the cares of Government released,
>   Our Indian governors their ease enjoy,
> In pleasures, by the contrast – much increased
>   Their intermediate moments they employ.'[2]

NOTES

1.   Graham, Maria. 1813. Journal of a Residence in India. George Ramsay and Company.

2.   D'Oyly, Charles.1828. Tom Raw, The Griffin: A Burlesque Poem, In Twelve Cantos: Illustrated By Twenty-Five Engravings, Descriptive of The Adventures of A Cadet In The East India Company's Service, From The Period of His Quitting England To His Obtaining A Staff Situation In India. R. Ackermann.

FURTHER READING

Anabel Loyd	*Vicereine: The Indian Journal of Mary Minto*, Academic Foundation 2016
Anne de Courcy	*The Fishing Fleet: Husband Hunting in the Raj*, Phoenix 2012
Anne de Courcy	*The Viceroys Daughters: The Lives of the Curzon Sisters*, Phoenix 2001
Anne Thackeray, Richie Richardson	*Lord Amherst and the British Advance Eastwards to Burma*, Oxford 1919
Augustus Hare	*The Story of two Noble Lives: Being memories of Charlotte, Countess Canning and Louisa, Marchioness of Waterford*, G. Allen 1893
Charles Allen	*A Glimpse of the Burning Plain: Leaves from the Indian Journals of Charlotte Canning*, Michael Joseph 1987
Charles D'Oyly	*Tom Raw the Griffin*, R. Ackermann 1828
David Gilmour	*Curzon Imperial Statesman*, Farrar, Straus and Giroux 1994
David Gilmour	*The Ruling Caste: Imperial Lives in the Victorian Raj*, Pimlico 2007
Deborah Cherry, ed	*The Afterlives of Monuments*, Routledge 2014
Eadaoin Agnew	*Imperial Women Writers in Victorian India: Representing Colonial Life, 1850-1910*, Palgrave Studies in Nineteenth-Century Writers 2017
Eleanor Eden, ed	*Letters from India by the Hon. E.E.*, Richard Bentley and Son 1872
Emily Eden	*Up the Country*, Createspace Independent Publisher 2017
Emma Roberts	*Notes of an Overland Journey Through France and Egypt to Bombay*, WH Allen 1841
Emma Roberts	*Scenes and Characteristics of Hindosthan*, WH Allen 1837
Eugenia W Herbert	*Flora's Empire British Gardens in India*, Allen Lane and Penguin Books 2013
Flora Annie Steel & Grace Gardiner	*The Complete Indian Housekeeper and Cook*, Heinemann & Co 1898

George Curzon	*British Government in India: The Story of the Viceroys and Government Houses*, Cassell & Co 1925
Jan Morris & Simon Winchester	*Stones of Empire: Buildings of the Raj*, Oxford University Press 1983
JP Losty	*Calcutta City of Palaces*, British Library 1990
JP Losty	*Picturesque Views of India: Sita Ram*, Roli Books 2015
John Bradley, ed	*Lady Mary Curzon-Lady Curzon's India-Letters of a Vicereine* Beaufort Books 1986
JGA Baird, ed	*James Andrew Broun Ramsay Dalhousie, Private Letters of the Marquess of Dalhousie*, William Blackwood and Sons 1910
Kathleen Blechynden	*Calcutta Past and Present*, Thacker, Spink & Co 1905
Lucy Peck	*Agra The Architectural Heritage*, Roli Books 2008
Marian Fowler	*Below the Peacock Fan: First Ladies of the Raj*, Penguin Books Canada 1987
Mark Bence-Jones	*Viceroys of India*, Constable Co 1986
Mark Bence-Jones	*Palaces of the Raj: Magnificence and Misery of the Lord Sahibs*, Routledge 2017
Mildred Archer	*Natural History Drawings in the India Office Library*, Her Majesty's Stat. Office 1962
Montagu Massey	*Recollections of Calcutta for Over Half a Century*, Thacker Spink and Co 1918
Nancy Mitford, ed	*Stanleys of Alderley: Letters 1851-65*, Hamish Hamilton 1968
Peter Quennell, ed	*Memoirs of William Hickey*, Century Publishing, London 1975
Philip Davies	*Splendours of the Raj*, Penguin Books 1985
Rev Caesar Caine, ed	*Barracks and Battlefields in India*, JC Chapman 1891
Sten Nilsson	*European Architecture in India 1750-1850*, Faber and Faber 1968
Thomas R Metcalfe	*Forging the Raj: Essays on British India in the Heyday of Empire*, Oxford University Press 2005
Vidya Dehejia & Allen Staley	*Impossible Picturesqueness: Edward Lear's Indian Watercolours, 1873-1875*, Columbia University Press 1989
Virginia Surtees	*Charlotte Canning Lady-in-Waiting to Queen Victoria and Wife of the First Viceroy of India 1817-1861*, John Murray 1975
WH Fitchett	*The Tale of the Great Mutiny*, Smith, Elder and Co 1902
William Dalrymple, ed	*Fanny Parks - Begums, Thugs and White Mughals*, Eland 2002